# Insight
## from My Life to Your Life

# Insight
## from My Life to Your Life

Smokin Joe

# INSIGHT FROM MY LIFE TO YOUR LIFE

*Scripture quotations are taken from the King James Version (KJV) and the New King James Version (NKJV) of the Bible.*

*iUniverse books may be ordered through booksellers or by contacting:*

*iUniverse*
*1663 Liberty Drive*
*Bloomington, IN 47403*
*www.iuniverse.com*
*1-800-Authors (1-800-288-4677)*

*ISBN: 978-1-4917-5549-5 (sc)*
*ISBN: 978-1-4917-5547-1 (hc)*
*ISBN: 978-1-4917-5548-8 (e)*

*Print information available on the last page.*

*iUniverse rev. date: 3/11/2015*

# PREFACE

I am compelled to give God special thanks, as he made it possible for me to achieve one of my goals. He knew before the world existed that greatness was brewing in the bowels of my belly, but he had to bring me low enough so I could see it within myself. I thank him for his love, which his Son expressed many years ago by dying on the cross for our sins—no matter what color we are. I can't forget about the Holy Spirit, which comforted me when I felt alone.

I also thank God for giving me hope and peace that passes all understanding and for helping me survive all my trials and tribulations, which made me what I am today. I thank him for putting within me fear, because that is the beginning of knowledge and wisdom, which help us understand his ways and not focus on our own. I thank him for choosing me to stand up for his righteousness. I thank him for guiding me on a journey that has so many ramifications, a system for which man's only solution is to turn to God. I thank him for strengthening me and allowing me to control my anger so that I will not bring harm to others. He is my protector!

I thank him for being patient with me when I didn't understand what patience was all about. I thank him for surrounding me with his angels, day in and day out. It would take more than a book to list all the things for which I owe God thanks. I thank him for loving me and for giving me the will to want to know him with a sincere heart.

I thank all my family and friends, who inspired me to do better. Whether their intentions were good or bad, they helped. I believe that every great friendship must have a strong foundation if it is to last. I thank my son, Jakeem L. Robinson, who opened up his heart to receive and believe, and who trusted in me when I didn't trust myself. I thank the army pleased. I can't say how long my mother dealt with this issue, but as I got older I noticed her split personalities. There were many times, year after year, when my mother wasn't herself. I'd look directly into her eyes, and it would seem as though something else had ahold of her and wouldn't let go. Many times when she was in this state, she would not respond when we spoke to her but stare elsewhere in a daze. There wasn't much that I could do beyond maintain my love for her. My mother was admitted into a halfway house on several occasions because of this issue. It made her seem crazy, mentally ill. For months, she would be fine, laughing and playing with us. Then suddenly, out of nowhere, this thing would come upon her and hold her captive for quite some time. Actually, it brought darkness to my whole family, because my mother was the light of our house. She always thought someone was out to get her for no reason. She believed a witch doctor could heal her from this sickness, and I often hoped he would. I guess my father hoped the same thing, because when my mother asked him to take her to the witch doctor, he did so without mumbling a word.

I do not want to exploit my mother and her issues, so if it seems that way, I apologize to my siblings. I just want people to know that even if a person has a mental illness, God is still in control. Filled with God's spirit, my mother did not harm her children, and it easily could have gone a different way. We cannot be afraid of the truth. I thank her for being a strong woman who endured everything life threw at her. Later on in life, my brother Willie told me what might have been the cause of her illness. He said my mother and her favorite sister got into an argument, and they didn't have the chance to apologize to each other, because the sister died. That destroyed my mother.

I love you, Carrie, with all my heart.

# CHAPTER 1

# Cedar Tree

Whatever we do, we should have self-control when doing it. The Lord knows what we will do even before we do it, so why not have some respect for God and stay within the boundaries. Sometimes that seem like a difficult task to accomplish, but through Christ Jesus, all things are possible.

One time my roommate, John, and I went to a nearby park to go jogging. As we began to jog, I saw a nice lady and her son throwing a softball back and forth. I waved to her, just to see if she would respond. And she did. My next move was to talk to her, since I didn't see a man around. But before I did, I argued within myself several times. I wasn't sure how she would react if I went over and interrupted her evening with her son. I finally got the courage and walked up and introduced myself. After we broke the ice, we talked about life. I could tell that she enjoyed the conversation, because when I first approached, she looked like she didn't want to be bothered. But after I told her that I was a true believer of God, she could tell I was being honest with her. And I did not get out of line and say crazy things, which also gave me some cool points. When I first walked over, she paid more attention to her son, as she should have; but before I left she wasn't throwing the ball to her son as much as she had been in the beginning. She was more interested in what I had to say and also wanted to add her opinion, which I thought was wonderful. We both learned something from each other. My point is, if she had not wanted to talk to me, my self-control would have kept me from getting angry or saying something stupid. I have seen people lose control just because a woman didn't like them. This control, which keeps you in line when things get out of hand, can be obtained only from God.

Love is a four-letter word that most times means more than what we may think. My brother Tony and I enjoyed playing pool at a sports bar called Temptation's. We also went there for the scenery it provided for any man who wanted to meet a nice-looking lady. When we went there, I often saw a high-yellow girl walking around, taking orders. I thought she was a beautiful woman. One day I told Tony that I was going to have her; be careful what you ask for, because it just might happen. My brother and I were just chilling and decided to shoot pool at Temptation's. I got up the nerve to ask her name and if I could get her phone number. When I approached, I must have startled her, because she looked a bit shaken up. She politely told me her name was Linda and gave me her pager number. I didn't care what number it was, as long as I had some way of getting in contact with her. I didn't want to take up much of her time because she was working.

I paged Linda a few times and took her to work. My feelings for her kept growing. Not long afterward, she agreed to go out on a date with me. We went to a club, and then Linda spent the night at my place. The next morning, she said she needed to leave and take care of something. I asked why she had to leave, because I was very interested in her, and I didn't want her to go just yet. Linda said she had an appointment with the cable company, and she didn't want to miss it. I had nothing else to say; I took her home as she'd asked. But I was a bit concerned, because something didn't feel right about the situation. It was that she was meeting the cable guy on a Sunday. I wasn't aware at that time that you could get cable hooked up on a Sunday.

About three days passed, and I didn't hear anything from Linda. On the fourth day, while I was at work, I got a call from my nephew Derrick. He said that Linda had called; she was in jail for writing a bad check. Somehow I thought it was my responsibility and obligation to visit her in jail. I know that most people would have a different opinion, but I liked her and wanted to give her a chance. On my third visit, I told Linda I loved her; my heart overpowered my mouth. I really don't know why I told her that, because I barely knew this woman. I'd like to believe that God had more to do with it than I did. I say that because Linda told me she'd felt like killing herself before I said I loved her. I do know that God placed me in Linda's life for a reason, even though our relationship didn't last long. Some may not understand why God allows us to cross paths with another person, which may cause us to stay too long and become trapped, especially when the other person has some issues, which may not be good. But God knows all our needs and the times when they need to be met.

I believed Linda needed a friend who would love her in a time of despair. God knew what she would face even before she did, and I came along in her life at the right moment. I can't speak for Linda, but I learned a valuable lesson from our relationship. I've learned how to love even more and to hold fast to that love, just as God loves me. The rest is up to the other person, who has to do their job and return the love. But you know what it is like when you first meet someone to whom you are attracted. It seems like they are the best thing ever to come into your life. With Linda, I wasn't sure if she were really my type. I didn't know exactly what I wanted; plus, I had no idea that my feelings for her would grow. I had rushed into my first marriage, so I didn't want to rush this relationship. But as I spent more time with Linda, it happened anyway. Still, I wanted to approach it from a different angle. I'd heard stories from guys who said that when you act like you don't care for a woman, she gives you all the respect in the world. And when you show her that you truly love her, that's when she gives you her ass to kiss. I used two tactics with this one lady and I was intrigued with both results.

The first tactic of being hard worked, although I didn't believe it would. I wasn't mean to Linda or anything like that; I just acted like I didn't care that much. In the beginning, she was all over me and wanted to be around me all the time. I felt like I was being crowded and my space was being invaded. But I enjoyed it as well; it felt good to have a woman chase me for a change. To be honest with you, at that time I had forgotten how to be in love; it had been more than fifteen years since my wife and I had separated. But trying to be hard core with Linda backfired on me like a rubber band that had been stretched to its greatest potential, and, in the end, the pain popped back at me. I fell deeper and deeper in love with her, while it seemed as though she was falling out of love with me, especially when word got out that I was still married. I tried to explain my reasons for not telling her, but she did not want to hear them. Here's a tip for women in general: if you want to know something, just ask. Linda didn't ask, so I kept my mouth shut.

I wasn't sure if we had the right chemistry. I knew that her love for me was weakening, because one time Linda and I got into an argument and she left. We were apart for no more than two weeks or so, but she had slept with someone else. I was torn apart. But I didn't want to give up on her, because I'd come to the conclusion that men had done the same thing to women for many years. I wanted to show her that I was a different type of man; I wasn't a man who would easily give up. But things didn't get any better. Meanwhile, we were still in this relationship.

I got her a car in my name, and by then I was all in. I wanted to marry Linda. For whatever reason, we stayed together. I changed from being that hard-core guy, and then I implemented the second tactic. I only wanted to give her my love. When we got mad, it sometimes lasted for days. I got fed up with the whole idea. It seemed like she didn't want to say anything to me, and when I said something to her, her attitude stunk. Sometimes that would last for three days or even more; when we went to bed, she slept close to the wall to keep from having to touch me, and I would get as far away from her as possible. We acted like two selfish children. Because I was older, I should have taken the situation by the horns and guided it into a different direction, but I didn't.

One night—the final night that Linda and I slept in the same bed—we were once again mad at each other, for no reason. That night, I believed God had to step in, because our time was up. When I got into bed, I noticed that Linda did not have on any clothes. It had been awhile since we'd had sex, but that night I wasn't that focused on sex, even though she was very enticing. As we relaxed in bed, Linda placed one of her soft and thick thighs across my body. Clearly, she was trying to have sex with me; I assumed it was her way of ending the feud between us. I didn't see it that way, so I pushed her leg off me. And she put her thigh on me once more. I wanted to talk about our problems, not just smooth it over with sex. The next morning, I suggested it might be better if she stayed with friends until things got better. I didn't want us to break up, but something had to give, because it was unhealthy for Linda and me to keep ignoring one another the way we were.

Linda wrecked the car I bought not long after I purchased it. In fact, she was in two wrecks. After we broke up, it took me awhile to get the car back. Even through all that, I still loved Linda. If that wasn't love, then I'm not sure what love is really about. Being an older man, I thought about our relationship and assumed that we did it all backward. Sex played a very big role in our relationship, but it only made us think that we were deep in love. We allowed the sex to overwhelm us. We didn't have the sense to take the time to become friends first and get to know one another. Tip: love can't be a one-lane road with two cars driving head-on. Devastation is bound to be the end result.

Love should conquer and destroy every vehement spirit that attempts to harm what God has put together. Love occurs when people are able to give and receive it. Love isn't about what someone can do for you, although some of us think it is. If God felt that way about us, then where would we be, because everything belongs to him. Think about that when you believe someone doesn't love you just because he or she doesn't give to you. They may not be able to give to you all the time, and if they could, they shouldn't anyway. That will only make that person hate you, which will give them the power to disrespect you. The only one you can love this much is God; now take that to the bank, and I promise that your interest will be great in time. "Because the foolishness of God is wiser than men, and the weakness of God is stronger than men" (1 Corinthians 1:25). Fight for love, so that you can love others as you love yourself. At times, people may not act the way you think they should, but God has a remedy for all illnesses. Oftentimes, for many different reasons, we get caught up in pretend love, and the consequences don't cross our minds. My relationship with Linda was doomed from the start. We didn't handle our situation properly; we were blind to reality.

The book of Isaiah describes how Isaiah had a vision: God had nourished and brought up his children, but they rebelled against him. God wanted Isaiah to tell them how he felt about their disobedience. "The ox knows his owner, and the ass his master's crib, but Israel doth not know, my people doth not consider" (Isaiah 1:3 KJV). God was saying that a four-legged animal knows who is in charge and respects his master's authority, and that a donkey—supposedly one of the world's stupidest animals—may have more sense than humans. It is terrible when we forget who created us. But God has a solution.

> And I will turn my hand upon thee, and purely purge away thy dross, and take away all thy tin: And I will restore thy judges as at first, and thy counselors as at the beginning: afterward thou shall be called, the City of Righteousness, the Faithful City. (Isaiah 1:25–26 KJV)

On one hand, God said that he was going to get rid of their worthless matter; perhaps he meant their privileges. On the other hand, he said he would strip them of their tin, that is, everything that they valued most. I know that feeling, and I am a witness to what God will take from you. Once we take our focus off God, we get complacent, forgetting our priorities and principles. The purging of my life woke me up to the reality of everything I was doing wrong. First my girlfriend left. Then I had to pawn almost everything I owned just to pay my bills. There were several times when I thought my car would get repossessed; I was behind on five months of payments. But I guess that God felt that he had taken away enough of my dross and alloy to set me on the path of righteousness.

Tragic things sometimes happen, and you may feel that they are unusual; for example, when you break up with someone. Remember, you are not the only one who has experienced this. But don't try to replace that empty space in your heart by quickly getting into another relationship. Sometimes it may work, but most of the times it won't. That person may turn out to be worse than the one you were with. What will work is asking God for help; he will guide you toward his wonderful knowledge. He is waiting on you. Forget about trying to get yourself right before you go to him; he says, "Come as you are." Even if you feel like you are nothing, God can change you into somebody. He will give you a peace of mind that passes all understanding. He will show you how to give and receive love. But you must show God that you love him, by doing what is right. Even when you get tired, never stop pushing, regardless of where you are or where you have been. I can't count the times I've wanted to throw in the towel, but something burning deep down inside will not allow me to give in.

Many people are waiting for someone else to be resurrected before they can be inspired. The more I read my Bible, the more I understand how it can help my life. I just hope that all people want to learn more about God's ways and not about the ways of the world. God helped me tremendously when I was going through some rough times I thought I wouldn't be able to bear. I was trying to find my way out of a jungle that refused to set me free. God shone a small light for me to follow—the vision of me writing this book—and will guide me to victory and the promise land. With God's help, we can find that place deep inside us and strive for greatness. Only God can reach that place and attach it to your heart and mind. He is the source that you must seek first.

One day I told God that I would not give up on finishing this book, no matter what. Many times I've wanted to eat those words and return them to the bowels of my belly, because I faced obstacles I thought I couldn't overcome. I wanted to change my direction and crawl into the hole of complacency, where I could be satisfied doing nothing to better myself. I knew that writing the book would be hard, especially dealing with everything else that was going on in my life, but I had no idea it would be this difficult. Over time, I learned that God doesn't ensure that everything we want to accomplish will be easily achieved. Oh, there will be challenges and great hills to climb. In other words, change doesn't always take place when we feel it should.

For example, one Sunday I walked outside to get some fresh air, because I hadn't made it to church. I had been in the house almost the whole day. I approached a nearby pond and sat on a bench, gazing at the ripples on the water. They appeared to be going backward and forward, but they actually were only going forward. I compared my life to the ripples in the pond; there were many similarities. My life had many setbacks that resembled the ripples in the pond; they appeared to be moving backward when they were moving forward. Likewise, I was able to move ahead in time, with faith and hard work.

Satan loves to conspire and plot when it comes to the truth about God. He wants us to think that we are moving backward when we are actually moving forward. We don't help the situation if we get angry with God when things don't go the way we want them to. Now, I know ripples on the water are caused by gravity and the moon rotating around the earth's surface, but my subconscious makes me think some of them are moving backward. My point is, we can't move forward if we feel like we are going backward most of the time. A washing machine, for example, moves back and forth until the clothes are clean. A car will not move unless the pistons go up and down. Only when we understand that our lives go through this same process of cycles will we realize that we are always moving forward. But we must show some type of action.

Don't forget—there will always be ripples in our lives, like the waves in a pond or an ocean. There may be long intervals between them, but we must keep cycling through. We need to focus our eyes, find the devil that corrupts our minds, and flush him out.

The ways of God and the ways of this world are very different; although, it is hard to distinguish between the two at times. The ways of the world take your mind off the important things in life, and the ways of the Lord put your mind at ease so you can see what is important. The craziest thing is you won't realize it until you are knee-deep in crap, especially if you are happy with the ways of the world. That is the difference in how the world perceives life and how God's creation was meant to be. Neglect is one way the world has of putting you in a place of misery. But having God as our friend as well as our Savior encourages us to look at ourselves in the mirror, as though we were watching a movie with mystery and drama. A good movie is captivating; it is hard to get up, because we don't want to miss any part of the story. And sometimes we can predict what is about to happen.

God shows us how things may play out in our own lives when we defy him. Unfortunately, the world may convince you that everything is just fine. The world uses its desirable beauty to camouflage its evil, and the reality is not revealed until after you fall, making you less concerned about the beauty of the Lord. "Buy the truth, and sell it not; also wisdom, instruction, and understanding" (Proverbs 23:23 KJV). This verse means there is a price we must pay before we can inherit the truth. There are many different ways of paying off this debt and reclaiming this truth, which prophets have known about since way before our time. You must be willing to sacrifice something for God, and not just any old thing. Praying is a good start; it allows God to begin his work and open up your mind. Meditating on God delegates his thoughts and brings us into his control. These days, sacrifice is rarely used to pay off the debt. I wouldn't depend on it being the only thing to save my soul, because my sacrifice may not please God or I might sacrifice for the wrong reason. I want to make this clear: This is just my opinion about sacrifice, and you have to discern things for yourself. However, sacrificing does help you in many ways. "Offer the sacrifices of righteousness, and put your trust in the Lord" (Psalm 4:5 KJV). Being patient is a great sacrifice, and it consists of waiting for something that may not happen when you think it should. God waited seven days to form heaven and earth when he could have done it in a matter of seconds. That tells us we must be patient and that wisdom, instruction, and understanding are a trinity and triumph; there can't be one without the others. Unless you learn them, where will truth reside in you? Those are just a few of the things you can do to pay our debt, and we all are a part of one another. One man can't do this alone; we need each other's energy to keep our bodies alive, and we are the body of Christ.

One night I was studying the Bible; afterward I had a strong urge to write about a bug that was walking around the lightbulb hanging from my ceiling. It didn't seem to have any sense of direction of where it wanted to go. I didn't write that night because I allowed things in my life to distract my thoughts and take me away from writing. But the very next night I was compelled to write about the great knowledge God was pouring into my soul and mind, because there was another bug walking around the light, same as the first one had done. But I noticed that the first bug from the night before wasn't moving at all; I assumed it had died from the heat of the bulb. Evidently, it didn't know how to separate itself from the heat of light. And as I looked at the second bug, it too was headed down the same path. This is where human pride kicks in, preventing knowledge from entering people's hearts. In the end, we are no different from these two bugs; one saw the other walk around the lightbulb and followed suit.

The other day, as I was walking, two young girls were riding their bikes. As they passed me, they split up; one went over the grass and the other went on the driveway. The one who rode on the grass told the other girl to come her way, and her friend said, "I thought we weren't supposed to ride on the grass." The other said, "Everyone does it." And the friend turned around and followed, even though she knew it was wrong. There is nothing wrong with someone who loves you showing you the way to do things. But you still must have a mind of your own. They can put you on the right path, but they can't take you to the end of the path. Why is it so hard for us to hear and do what God wants instead of being a slave to man's way? Think about this for a moment. We all have shortcomings, but some people have way more than others. It is not for us to judge, but we can learn from the mistakes of others. Why do the same things they have done and limit your options as well?

Another point about those bugs: they were probably cold and, attracted by the heat of the bulb, they got comfortable. We often get comfortable, which can turn into complacency, and in various situations that can have a tremendous effect on our life. Having one thought in our minds too long makes it easier for Satan to stick his fork in us. An idle mind is the devil's workshop. Here is a list of a few things that will bring your life to a halt and throw your mind off those things you want to accomplish: not wanting to know the truth about God, laziness, robbery, theft, hatred, envy, pride, obsession, worrying, and unrequited love. All these factors can be instruments of mass destruction, but there is one that I am inspired to write about—obsession; plus, I thought it might help some young men in the future.

I had a classmate, John, back in grade school with whom I played basketball from time to time. But when we got into the seventh or eighth grade, he moved away. Then about two years later, he had returned—with height. Before he moved, I had no problem beating him in a pickup game. With his new height, I had no chance unless I learned a new strategy, but my game had remained the same. John became popular for playing high school basketball. When he played, I saw something in him that was worth molding and taking to the next level. I only wish he could have seen it in himself. Most of the time, it happens that way—we can't see greatness in ourselves. John ended up meeting this nice-looking girl at our school after he returned. They got married, even though he was about to go to college. John's marriage wasn't such a bad thing, but it made him let go of everything else, including his dreams of going to college and playing pro basketball. I understand that we all have to make our own decisions. I had to make decisions on my own, and a lot of them were bad. But I believe that this woman was a big obsession and distraction for John, and I felt like it kept him from going to college. If she truly loved him, she would have supported him and would not have torn him down.

One night I went to the club, where I happened to see John and his wife. There was this guy standing among the crowd of people on the dance floor. When John and his wife walked in, the guy grabbed John's wife on her butt, and the only thing she did was look back and smile. It seemed like she enjoyed it; in fact, I know she did. Any real woman would have said something to her husband. Some women may say that she was probably trying to protect him by not saying anything. Try selling that story to *Ripley's Believe It or Not!* Yes, if she'd said something, it could have started a fight, but that would show her loyalty. John could have made it with his basketball skills if he had remained focused. I believe! I encourage you to do something constructive before you try to build a family; don't do what everyone else does. I think that John did what most people do; he fell in love, got married, and fell out of love at a young age. And I had done the same like most people.

The Bible is very interesting because God provides the meaning of some of the scriptures right away. Take, for example, Luke 8:12 (NKJV): "Those by the wayside are the ones who hear; then the devil comes and takes away the word out of their hearts, lest they should believe and be saved." Jesus was saying that people hear the word of God but are easily influenced by temptations from Satan. Let's say you decide to give your life to God; then someone else tells you to change. Usually this is someone close to you. Just as God can use one person to tell another a life-changing word, Satan can as well, but nothing will change. Anything that has to do with doing right and the truth about God doesn't necessarily have to come from the Bible. Information received via word of mouth can lead to redemption. You may not see it at first; it may take some time before God moves on your behalf. He first has to prepare you for what he has in store for your life. Just take a step back and know that you are already blessed, regardless of your current situation. The Lord allows us to see the godless side of the world and the zeal of his love for us. Which will you choose? The verse mentioned above strengthens those who refuse to believe that God is not real. Satan tries to trick us into believing that God will not do what he says he will do for us. It's like having bait on the line to catch a fish, and Satan's bait to catch a man can be enticing.

Another way that Satan can take the word out of your heart is by using someone else to patronize you and keep his foot on you, especially when you don't know any better. It is just as easy for God to convert us as it is for Satan to mess us up and confuse us. We should rejoice in the Lord. "Submit yourselves therefore to God. Resist the devil, and he will flee from you" (James 4:7 KJV). If we totally submit ourselves to God, he will be more willingly to show us how the devil attacks us. And, yes, Satan will leave for a moment, but he also will return with a vengeance. Satan can't do anything you don't permit with your mind and tongue. "They on the rock are they, which, when they hear, receive the word with joy; and these have no root, which for a while believe, and in time of temptation fall away" (Luke 8:13 KJV). These are the people who at first have faith and believe that God is real, but they only take a good sermon to heart for a while. As soon as they walk out the church doors, their faith vanishes like thin air. We listen to the Word of God so we can embed it deep in our hearts and no one or nothing can root it up. You may feel like you are connected to God, but as soon as Satan is present, you backslide. Even longtime Christians can be tempted and sometimes fall. But they know how to get back into right standing with God and ask for forgiveness. Don't let anything pull you out so far that you can't ask God to forgive you. Sex, money, and drugs are three of mankind's main temptations; they may open up many more doors, allowing Satan to come in and destroy whatever you may be trying to build. Of course, this includes married couples who play the cheating game; the pain can be much more severe. Things do get crazy, and one may try to blame the other so that he or she feels justified. Take Adam and Eve; when Eve encouraged Adam to take from the tree of good and evil, God didn't punished just one; both suffered. We, however, hate to get involved when the law asks us to testify.

I once was tempted by a woman I had met through an online dating service. I'd told her that I was a minister before we met. But after I took her out on a date and we returned to her house, she seemed as though she didn't care that I was a minister, because she went on about sex as if it were going out of style. She asked me to go upstairs and move a television for her. At first, I didn't think anything of it, but seconds later, I came to my senses. I assumed that this woman was trying to get me up to her room and who knows what else may have happened. The funniest thing was that I had not planned to meet this woman just to have sex with her. I'd hoped that we'd have some things in common. At that point in my life, I was very stern about not falling into temptation, and I kept a good handle on things.

Back then I would have said that if you were committed to God then you had to be faithful to him, no matter what. I would have promised that you would not fall into temptation. Today, I have a different perspective because I have since fallen—not because I was tempted, but because I wanted it, I felt I needed to. If there were consequences, I was ready for them. I realized over the years that temptation will come, but we must do as the Bible says:

> Fight the good fight of faith, lay hold on eternal life, whereunto thou art called, and hast professed a good profession before many witness. (1 Timothy 6:12 KJV)

> And that which fell among thorns are they, which, when they have heard, go forth, and are choked with cares and riches and pleasures of this life, and bring no fruit to perfection [maturity]. (Luke 8:14 KJV)

Many of us think that money brings the full capacity of happiness. If that were true, why would so many people with money turn to drugs? Yes, it is true that poor people are also hooked on drugs. But let's keep our attention on the fact that money isn't always the key to an abundant life. The reason why we are choked by the pleasures of life is because we love to satisfy our lust. How can you bring anything to a level of perfection without doing it over and over again? Once you learn how to harvest fruit at its ripest stage, you know what it takes to do it again. Many people hear the Word of God but don't grab hold to the true meaning of it. In the book of Ecclesiastes, Solomon said that he had everything, from riches to women, and he searched out all things under the sun, and all was vanity. Everything that he had seemed to be more than it really was. I'm sure he also wondered how money could bring destruction to people who say they love each other. How could a woman birth a child and then kill it? Why does love hurt so badly? After you give your best to another, how can they treat you like crap? How can people talk to your face, smile, and then turn right around and talk about you behind your back? These are just a few

wrong way. People, we must learn that God is not pleased with us when we find ourselves doing the same thing over and over again, especially when it doesn't pertain to his righteousness. And once we have gotten caught in a trap, we want his forgiveness and healing. Many times we override what is right; when we do, we have to get back on the bull with dignity and strive once again to be what God expects us to be. Brad ended up losing his house while he was in school trying to better himself. He had a job driving for the Metropolitan Atlanta Rapid Transit Authority (MARTA), and he made decent money. I can't legitimately say this was the reason why this happened to him, but it is food for thought. And there is nothing wrong with trying to better yourself. I believe that if Brad weren't so narrow-minded about the righteousness of God, he would not have been emasculated in the mind. Our thoughts and decisions about God influences how God gives us his knowledge, wisdom, and understanding that allows him to do more than what we ask of him. If there were any other way to get people to open their eyes and think about how the things they say and do determine how their life might be in the future. We don't often sit back and observe ourselves to see how our faults cause pain to others and ourselves. But we are quick to point fingers at someone else. God is so amazing, he gave us enough knowledge to survive on this earth. He knew that if he allowed us to obtain too much knowledge, we wouldn't know what to do with it; we'd just destroy ourselves. Why judge another if you can't judge yourself? I can attest to these things because I had to judge myself so I could see my faults.

Many people talk about God, but do they really know him? They may have known him, but with their disobedience have fallen from his grace. So do you think they still know him? I wouldn't want to lose my relationship with God due to stupidity. One day while I was going to work, I noticed this older guy walking. I felt sympathy for him and decided to offer him a ride. After he got into my car, the gentleman told me that he didn't stay too far from where I picked him up. We began to drive toward his living quarters and got on the subject of the Bible. He told me that he once was on a quest for God, back in the day. He took many trips all over the world. What was an eye-opener for me was that this guy was drinking a beer and said it was okay to go to strip clubs; God would understand. I felt that was a bit bizarre and sinful, maybe because I wasn't doing either of those things. And I sure didn't believe that God would understand. (Since I gave my life to God, I have been to a strip club once. I'm not saying that it was the right thing to do; I just want you to know that even when I think I am in control, there is no telling when I may choose to lose my focus and purpose. And I can't sit here and say that God understands why I did what I did.) Anyway, this man asked if I wanted to come up to his place and read some of the books he had collected over the years. I didn't take him up on the offer because I didn't feel that would give me the knowledge I needed to move closer to the Lord. My time in the ministry was relatively new, so I thought Satan was trying to corrupt my mind through this man. Maybe he had fallen from God's grace. But who was I to judge? We can never know all of God's thoughts.

I have wanted to quit this journey many times, and writing this sometimes gave me that extra urge to quit. For some reason, the inner part of me—which must be God's Holy Spirit—won't allow it. Once I walked about fifteen miles from work because my roommate Dan forgot to pick me up. After awhile, I felt like I had no legs. I wanted to quit so much. But that spirit within me said I could make it, even though my limbs gave off a different signal. My goal was to make it home in a certain period of time and if I had stopped it would have delayed my arrival. The other reason why I wanted to stop was that my feet were hurting, like I'd run a marathon. Making it home and getting into bed before it got too late kept me pushing. We must set goals for ourselves and strive for them. That gives us the extra motivation to complete the task. When God deals with us, he uses some of these same approaches to finish the job. I know some of you don't like your current situations. But to move elsewhere in life, you must go through some pain. I had to walk those fifteen miles to get home, but after I got home, the pain was gone. The only thing I felt was joy. You too can make it home by listening to the spirit of the Lord and following through with your goals.

Here is an example of one of my goals and the strength behind it that keeps me pressing: I hope that one day I won't have to work for someone else and can be my own boss. I can't stand how some supervisors act like you are nothing and you don't even exist. Make sure you stay in the good soil; he will help you grow in many facets of your life.

# CHAPTER 2

# Bodhi Tree

Don't let life's circumstances get you to the point where you have no control of your thoughts. Take control of them. One day, I was talking to my son, Jakeem, about different issues that people face and the way those problems make you feel. He said, "You can lock me up, but you can't lock up my mind." I found this very intriguing and inspiring. I didn't know exactly what made him say that; at the time, he was only eleven years old. I was proud of my son for saying those powerful words and keeping them dear to his heart. If an eleven-year-old could adjust his mind when things didn't look right or feel good, then I wanted to encourage all young men with sons to push harder to show them you love them. Wherever you are right now, express your love for your son. You may not have been there for him as a father should be, but don't let that stop you. When you go to him, be sure you do what you say. And sons, receive your fathers with open hearts. God will see you both through.

My reason for taking time to write about this subject is because there were times when I wasn't there for my son. And the way he felt during those years of my absence have weighed on my shoulders. I felt like a grain of sand, knowing that I had a son who needed me, but didn't have his father. I didn't want to be around my son just because his mother didn't want to be with me, and I know now that it was a childish reason. Because I wasn't thinking properly, my son experienced some awful things at a young age. I can't change the past and the things that my son had to face, but you can make a change now for your child. You don't have to wait years down the line and then try to make it up. Tomorrow is not promised to anyone. If you act now, you may stop your son from joining a gang or committing suicide. We need to come at this issue from a different angle, so that our sons can learn to become real men.

Satan will entice them to do the opposite of the good advice you may be giving them. My father used to tell all his children to save money. You would think he made his point clear by saying it over and over again. We probably heard him make this statement at least once a month, maybe more. It was nerve-racking and didn't mean anything to me back then. But he wasn't saying it to get on our nerves; he was telling us for our own good. I guess I didn't listen because he never explained why it was so important to save money. I gathered a lot of my habits from my mother, since I was around her most of the time. And she was not good about holding on to money. I realize now that when people love you, they will tell you things for your own good; hopefully they can explain it so you can grasp hold of what they are saying. But it is up to the child to take in the information that is being provided to them. And please explain to them why it is important.

It is very essential for you to step up and be a better father to your son. When the enemy gets ahold of him, there may not be any hope of getting him back. If you don't stand up now and decide to be a more effective father, you will feel like less of a man in the future. I can't speak for all men, but I know what happened to me when I wasn't the father I needed to be toward my son. I felt guilty. I asked myself why I didn't spend more time with him. Just because you feel you have failed doesn't mean you have to give up. When you give up, your son feels as though he should give up as well. Try again, but try harder and put more effort in it. My son asked, "Why doesn't my father want to come see me? What have I done wrong?" He wondered many times whether he was the reason I'd left his mother. If you love your child but act like a fool, as I did, for whatever reason, you can only blame yourself when he becomes rebellious and mischievous. Fathers need to protect their children from Satan's truculence and his eagerness to quarrel with your sons' premature minds. We need to be there for them and teach them the way of the Lord, before they are released into the wild. Satan is eager to snatch up your boys who have neither leadership nor guidance from men who live for righteousness; he will stick his forks into their sides and will devour them.

Do not always look for the negative sides of things; focus on the positive. For instance, let's say your girlfriend left you for another man. Be glad that she did, because evidently she wasn't right for you in the first place. "While we look not at the things which are seen, but at the things which are not seen: for the things which are seen are temporal; but the things which are not seen are eternal" (2 Corinthians 4:18 KJV). This whole father topic makes me think about an old friend named Ken. When I was in the army, almost every time I came home, someone told me Ken had another child on the way. And the government was cracking down on men thought to be deadbeat dads. If you don't protect yourself, you will be hurt in the long run. In addition, you will reach a point when you'll be unable to care for all those kids.

My son came to live with me for about two weeks one summer. And when I took him back home, his cousin, who happened to be Ken's son, was there as well. I asked him when he'd last seen his father, and he said, "About two years ago." I felt sorrow for the young man, because in my eyes his father was a good guy. But as I was leaving, the boy grabbed my arm and said that I was his dad. I didn't know what to say, but he really touched my heart. I believe that is my worst fear—for my son to call another man Dad. That was why it was important to show my son that I could be the caring father he desired me to be. What was unusual about my son's cousin was that I had never taken him anywhere or done anything for him; yet he said I was his dad. A child can learn to love and respect his father whether or not you have something for him; keeping in touch can only help. If you are able do something nice occasionally to gain his trust that is a plus. When you don't have any material goods, give him something no one can take away—the knowledge and love of God.

I'd always heard that God works in mysterious ways; then one day I experienced that for myself. My oldest brother, Willie, who was staying with me at the time, decided to move back to New Mexico. This news came as a shock to my ears, because things weren't going too well for either of us at the time. I didn't think he would leave me in that situation. But whatever his reasons for leaving, I had to live with them, stand up for myself, and be a responsible man. It didn't sit well with me, but all I could do was be strong. About six months earlier, my brother had applied for a job at an upholstery factory. The owner said he would call the next Friday, but he never did. The night before Willie was to leave, I prayed and asked God to give my brother a sign so that he would stay, but my brother's mind was made up to move back to New Mexico. Sure enough, the owner of the upholstery place called the following day before he left.

I did not believe I could handle things on my own, but God put a plan in place. Earlier, I'd been talking to my coworker Dave about my brother's plans to move back to New Mexico. Dave was a part of God's plan. He and I also talked about life and God every time we saw each other. We were both going through breakups at the time as well. Dave had no problem being my roommate once my brother was gone, although, as it turned out, he was only there for a short period of time. The fact remains that God was standing in my corner and waiting with what I needed to return to the battle.

Do people understand the difference between helping someone and hurting them? Let me explain. During my military service in Fort Bragg, North Carolina, I fell in love with a young lady named Savant. When it was almost time for me to leave that base and go to the next one, Savant, who had feelings for me as well, said I could stay with her until my North Carolina tour was over. She said it would help me save some money, so I took her up on the offer. Unfortunately, Savant didn't know what she wanted and that created problems. I'd asked if she wanted to move with me, but my brother Tony changed my mind about that decision, and that was a good thing. For one, she was still married, and two, she was a woman who liked sleeping with a lot of different men. She was very promiscuous, and I fell for her. Several things proved that she preferred more than one man.

Here is one example: The day I moved my things into her place, I already knew things would not go the way I wanted them to. I expected her to have another man come to the house after a few days, but not on the first day I moved in! I also wondered if I could overcome the resentment I had for her. About 7:00 or 8:00 p.m., an older guy and his woman came over to visit Savant; she said they were her cousins. Of course, I didn't believe that lie for one minute. While they were standing outside talking, I noticed the older gentleman flashing some money around as if he wanted Savant to see it. I sat in the house, waiting to see what would happen. After awhile, Savant took a walk with these people, and I waited a long time for her to return. I was hoping that she'd come back, get into the bed with me, and top the night off with some steamy sex. I must say that was one thing she was good at.

It got very late, and I didn't want to wait up for her anymore, so I decided to lie down in her bed. She also had a second room that was empty. While I was lying there, I thought about going into the other room and seeing what would happen when she came home. I wondered if she would come into the room where I was sleeping and tell me to lie down with her or if she'd have another man to fill that position. I moved to the other room, lay on the floor, and kept the door cracked just a bit. The suspense nearly killed me. I could not sleep, wondering if this lady would use her capabilities to put a dagger in my heart. Around 2:00 a.m., I heard her walking in and whispering to someone else. Then she closed the door of my room tighter, went into her room, and turned on the music so I couldn't hear anything. But I really didn't have to hear anything to know what was going on. My assumptions about this situation were on point from the start; it was like sinking the eight ball into the corner pocket. It is a sure winner!

That morning, about 5:00 a.m., I gathered my belongings and moved back to my crib, because I hadn't turned in the key just yet. Even though Savant believed she was helping me, she ended up hurting me in the process. She would have helped me more by not inviting me to stay with her, unless we'd been the only ones in the house. Once I left, she could've invited whomever she wished. Savant knew that I had feelings for her, and yet she slept with another man while I was there. That was not helpful; it was pernicious, harmful, and evil. Some of you may say, "I bet he wasn't saying that about her while they were having sex." I won't lie; that is true. But it still is inappropriate to sleep with one man while another man who has feelings for you is in the next room. She could have showed some respect until I was gone for good.

When you are doing those things that God has placed in your heart, he will speak to you at any time of the day. It could be early in the morning; he may wake you up to give what you need to enhance your vision. One night, God woke me up and told me to write in my book. It had been a good while since I'd last written in it. He said, "If you don't write in it this very moment, you will not remember what I am saying to you tomorrow morning." I didn't feel like writing, but the thoughts that God were revealing to me were so strong, I had no choice but to make them plain on paper. Many of us miss seeing the glory of God because we are careless and don't take action when we should.

Take, for example, Moses, who led the people of Israel out of the wilderness. They were supposed to be in the wilderness for only eleven days; instead they were there for forty years. The people complained about the things they had to face and said that they should have stayed where they were—in a place of bondage. God is speaking to many of you who are reading this book. He wants to bless you in every aspect of your lives, but many of you are too scared to stand up for his righteousness. You can't worry about what someone else will think; God is instructing you. How can we not believe that God won't bring our desires to pass when we diligently seek after him. The beginning of Genesis states that God made heaven and earth. If God brought heaven and earth into existence, then surely he can bring about a change in your life. Stop comparing man to God; no part of the Bible claims that man has that much power. God's Word can reveal every little thing that runs through the mind and can even calm you about the things he doesn't want us to know. You won't know this unless you seek out God for yourself. I have made some mistakes, and I had to reach out to God to turn my situation around. God will show himself in many different ways to get your attention after you make so many mistakes, you have no idea which way to turn. You may lose everything that you own; that could be his way of humbling you to learn about him. He will show you many signs that can prick your spirit, which knows who God is. God wanted me to share with his people, that night that he awakened me, that when he moves, we should move along with him as well. How can we hold onto his unchanging hand if we do not move? When we move with God, we are protected from the enemy.

One evening Willie was telling me how God wanted his people to live. That very night God was moving. I didn't take it seriously enough, but I knew that God was moving. Eventually, I had no choice but to take it to heart with mind, body, and soul. And God gave me a snippet of what my life would be like if I didn't follow him. I could have lost everything, which wasn't much from the start. My laziness would have made me even lazier. The direction I was headed was nowhere near the path he wanted me on.

The things with which I was dealing would have overtaken me with ease. Giving up would have been my only option for succeeding.

Here is another example of the way God deals with us and our problems. I was riding in my car one night, looking through the sunroof of my car, and I saw this airplane. At that time, I had been thinking about a terrible situation that was going on in my life. As I gazed at the plane for a while, God began to send his wonderful thoughts to my mind, bringing me peace. We all know that a plane moves very fast, but from the ground, it seems to be moving as slow as a turtle. It can travel through rain, sleet, or snow. God moves in our lives in the same way. With patience, we will get to where he wants us to be. Many people don't have patience to think that way. God didn't give us a mind so we would focus on the bad things when he is the pilot. Think about this for a moment. Wasn't there a time when you were suffering and you didn't know what to do or who to turn to? Just think about how God brought you out. Yes, it took time. Did you give him the credit?

God is expanding faster than your mind could ever imagine; he wants to bless you in many different ways. The reason things may not be going the way you think they should be is the fact that he may want you to slow down and take care of your current responsibilities. If you say that God is in control, then allow him to lead you. Sit there and meditate on where he has brought you. God has guided me through a long and winding road. Knowing that is what keeps me pushing to do better every day.

I used to work for a company called Anixter. For the first four months, my supervisor had me cutting different lengths of cable. The guy who was working on the manifest line quit, and they put me in his place. I was glad to have that position because it made me feel more important, and it had more responsibilities as well. The training they gave me was poor, but I managed to do my best. Not long after being placed in this position, I made a mistake by sending the product to the wrong place. I had a difficult time because I was doing four different jobs: cutting cable, packing, pulling orders, and manifesting. That was too much work for one person to handle, especially when I wasn't properly trained. Several days after my first mistake, I made the same mistake again. My supervisors gave me a verbal warning and said if it happened again, they would write me up. The third time it happened, they would fire me, no questions asked. From that day forward, when I went to work I was afraid. I wondered when I would make the next mistake that would cause me to lose my job. It was only a matter of time before it happened. If I lost this job, it would set me back, and I was trying to move forward.

Sometimes things are inevitable, but you never know that until after the fact. I understood very well that they would have to fire me if my work wasn't satisfactory. When God closes one door, he opens another one—but you have to believe that he will.

One day, someone pulled an order for me to ship out. As I was about to check the boxes to see if the products were in the boxes, the urge to do so vanished. Suddenly, it seemed as though someone were standing next to me, demanding that I stop checking the boxes and refrain from making sure all the products were there. There were two boxes in this particular order, and there should have been three items in each box. As the boxes came down the conveyor belt, it seemed that neither one had been opened. The person who packed the boxes should have left them open to let the next person on the assembly line know how many items were inside. But whoever packed this order either didn't care or was setting me up to get fired. I'd had some problems with my supervisor in the past; I suspected that it was him. Don't get me wrong. I knew that the blame rested with me if I didn't check the boxes. Whenever you think, *why is this terrible thing happening to me*, God will make a new thing take its place.

When I arrived at work the next morning, I didn't hear anything negative about the shipment. But later on, around 3:00 p.m., almost two hours before clocking out, I was called into the office. I already knew why they wanted me in the office. I thought that if they knew I'd made a mistake and were going to fire me, they should have done so that morning. The manager said I didn't send the right amount of items in that order. I was very upset when I heard this because I had been trying to get myself back on my feet after my stupidity.

Well, I was out of work again, but I kept my eyes focused on God, knowing and believing that he would come through for me. As I mentioned before, sometimes bad things happen, but with God on your side, things will work out in your favor eventually. If I had checked those boxes, God would never have moved me. He knew that I was being treated unfairly, and that was why he moved me, I think so!

Satan tries to confuse us about God. "If God is for us, who can be against us?" (Romans 8:31 NKJV). To be led by God, you have to get to know him. Start by getting into his Word, and wait until you get a revelation of his Word. Only you know how much darkness you are facing, and to hear someone talk about the goodness of God should be a blessing to you. Many people are lost without guidance from God, and they are not sure if they want to live or die. There are times when the situation gets so bad we don't want to do what is right, because we feel it is too hard to deal with. I've learned it becomes easier if you are willing to keep God's commandments.

During my search for this new job, one uncomfortable incident after another kept happening in my life. They didn't feel good at all, but I kept putting my trust in the Lord. Several months passed, and I was still seeking a job. I worked for a temp service I'd worked for in the past, which sent me to a company called Panasonic that distributed electronics. I had worked there for about four weeks, and then the project was over. I decided to call them back and see if they were looking for help. Every time I called, they said they didn't have any work, but to keep checking with them periodically. And I did so until one day when they asked if I knew how to drive a forklift. I knew right then that God had answered my prayers. Ironically, I'd received my certification to drive a forklift on my previous job. It is overwhelming to me how God moves me from one place to the next. The temp-service personnel manager asked me to come in for an interview; without hesitating, I jumped at the opportunity. When he interviewed me, he talked about the overtime I would get if I wanted to work. To be honest, the overtime didn't mean that much to me. I was glad to be working, even though it wasn't full-time. Don't give up on God or yourself.

David, my roommate, said that the company might hire me on a full-time basis. I told him that that would never happen; other temps had been working there longer than I had. David said, "Don't look at it that way." I took his advice and never looked back. Every day I went to work; being productive was the only thing on my mind. I wasn't worried at all about getting on full-time; I just wanted to show these people that I had no problem working. If they decided to hire me, they would know what kind of employee they were hiring. One day, I noticed a sign that said the company would be hiring people soon; résumés were requested by the following Monday. It never crossed my mind to apply because I thought I had no chance. I had only been there for a few months. That Saturday, we had to work, and one of the head supervisors called me into his office. I had no idea why he needed me; I knew I hadn't done anything wrong. When I walked in, he asked if I'd turned in a résumé. I asked, "For what?" He said if I wanted a job, I needed to hand in a résumé on Monday. I was impressed at the way God was moving in my life because of my faith and obedience to him. I was astounded to learn that some employees had to wait at least a year before getting hired full-time. God will take you from the bottom and place you on the top, if you put him first. He is the head and not the tail.

Let me tell you how people are about helping others. My license had been suspended, and I was unable to drive my car. I tried to do the right thing by not driving it. In the past, I had no fear about driving with a suspended license, but I had to end that bad habit. I wanted to ride with someone else to keep from getting into deeper trouble. I had been riding with Mr. Brown, an older coworker, for about a week. I asked Mr. Brown to drop me off at the exit to my house, but I still had to walk at least five miles to get home. It took him no more than one minute to pull off the road, let me out, and get back on the interstate. I told Mr. Brown that I would pay him on Friday for giving me a ride. That Friday, David picked me up from work because I wanted to be at church early; it was the last night for revival, and I wanted to be there on time. I didn't suspect that there would be any harm if I left and did not take care of Mr. Brown; I assumed I could pay him on Monday when I came to work. Before I left, I asked the supervisor to tell Mr. Brown I was leaving and would take care of him on Monday. Unfortunately, my message never reached him. I should have told him myself, and maybe things would have turned out differently. On Monday morning, I said, "Mr. Brown, I have not forgotten what I said I would give you for dropping me off." His reply was, "You disrespected me!" I couldn't believe what my ears were hearing. It wasn't that I didn't want to pay him; I was just in a hurry that Friday to get to church. I still believe if my supervisor had given him my message, there wouldn't have been a problem. Even when I tried to explain myself, Mr. Brown was adamant that I had disrespected him. We were both grown men and should have worked out the situation. I really needed that ride, like a cop needs his gun for a shoot-out. If you help someone else, it only comes back to you when you are in need.

I tried to plead with and convince Mr. Brown, but he didn't want to hear anything I had to say. He also told me that he wouldn't drop me off at the exit near my house anymore. But before this incident Mr. Brown and I had been talking, and he said if I became successful with my writing, he would be on my doorstep asking for money. And he meant what he said. I couldn't understand how he could turn his back on me but at the same time expect me to give him some of my earnings. I asked other guys to drop me off at this same exit, and they refused. Terry said his wife had been waiting outside for thirty minutes, and he needed to leave. And two other guys gave me lame excuses. Mind you, all these guys were African American, my own ethnicity. But I knew God would make a way out of no way. A young white guy named Tim, whom I had misjudged, took me all the way to my house without asking for one dime. We never know how God will work these things out for us, and it is very important to stay focused on him.

When I was in the fourth grade, I was kept back at the end of the year. At the beginning of the next school year, there was a girl named Janet who, for whatever reason, couldn't stand me. Whatever she had against me lasted until we were in high school. As far as I can remember, I didn't do anything to cause her to treat me so badly. At times, she called me all sorts of names, but I couldn't allow my heart to hate her. Hate is like a sponge that absorbs as much liquid as possible, but doesn't have a system in place for regurgitation. It cost me nothing to show love toward people without being concerned about the way they looked or anything else that may have made them stick out like a sore thumb. I am sure that helped me keep peace with Janet throughout those years. In the twelfth grade, I still kept my peace, but Janet had changed. That last year of school I sat right behind her and didn't know what to expect. I just kept to myself and didn't say anything. If she had something against me, it was best to stay silent. I couldn't stay silent for long, however, because I enjoyed singing, and right before class I'd sing in a low voice. I didn't care if Janet said something degrading to make me feel bad. Singing lifted me up when I was down; I enjoyed it with a passion. One day Janet asked, "Are you going to sing for me today?" I could not believe that Janet liked my voice. And she wasn't cruel to me. Instead she wanted to be my friend, after all those years of putting me down for no reason; she came to her senses and realized I was not an enemy. It made me feel good that Janet and I were finally getting along. In other words, always treat people the way you want to be treated; in the end, you will see the untold revelation of God's love.

God would wake me up early in the morning to write because I was more attentive to what he had to say. One morning God told me he wants to bless his people more than we think. But how is that possible when we won't get off our lazy behinds and do the work that is needed to get the job done. Since my walk with Christ, I've found out that it is a blessing to go through all these unyielding trials we face. They make us walk upright with God and do the things we normally wouldn't do. We receive blessings by standing up for something and passing tests. They are there to give us a jump-start and get us on the right path. Anytime you are striving to do right, God will reveal that you are headed in the right direction. The day I was writing in this book about jump-starting, my friend Dale told me that he had to jump-start someone's car. We all need a jump-start or a jolt from time to time. I can say from experience, without the bad things in my life, there is no way I would be where I am today. Satan comes to destroy, but God will restore.

There is a scripture that will help you prosper in your spiritual and physical lives: "Yea, a man may say, Thou hast faith, and I have works: show me thy faith without thy works, and I will show thee my faith by my works" (James 2:18 NKJV). Human beings can have all kinds of faith in their hearts, but if that faith is not in God, how can you work for God? The faith and works referred to by James are evidence that you are a believer in Christ. For a child of God, it impossible for faith to exist without the works. After you complete the work that God has given you, your faith will be evident; that is the proof that only God can strengthen you, through his power to complete the work.

For example, if things are not going so well in your life, allow God to take care of the situation, and do not do anything stupid to make it worse. If we believe that God will fix our problems in due time, he will increase his love for us. God wants us to think outside the box and know that he can do things that we never thought were possible. Many people don't want to think beyond their wildest dreams—not only do they refuse to believe a good thing might happen, they also don't want to work to ensure that it does. Trying to remain positive every day is a kind of work. Negativity is an energy that has to work alongside positivity, so when it comes, embrace it. To change your life from negative to fully positive, you need to know your status with the Lord, no matter what you may be up against. If you don't know, don't be afraid to ask him. Allow him to give you what you have been waiting for; then that void in your life can be filled with peaches and cream, a sensation that no human being can give you or take away. You can regain your joy and love, and your mind will be at peace. If you draw near to God, he will draw near to you. And when trouble arises, don't turn your back on God, because he may turn his back on you. If we strive to know him, I have faith that he will double his efforts to get us on the right path.

At times, God reveals he was blessing us even before we realized we needed him. He does this by showing us events that have already taken place. One Wednesday night, while I was in Bible study, one of the deacons read a scripture from Deuteronomy 28:3 (NKJV): "Blessed shall you be in the city, and blessed shall you be in the field." That passage made me think about when I was in the military. Even though we were training in the field, meaning the woods, we were still cared for the way we had been in the city. In the city, everything was more convenient, but I was blessed in the field as well. I woke up every morning with a sane mind. We ate morning, noon, and evening. We had light when we needed it. We think we are blessed only in the city because it has more to offer than the field. It is all about how you look at things. Later on in the service, the pastor talked about the military. That was God's way of showing me that I was blessed, even though I hated going to the field. It really doesn't matter where I am, I am still blessed. Remember, we can't allow our minds to conform to the ways of this world.

We think things should happen overnight, just because we give our lives to God. One night I felt a little weary about different situations in my life. After I went to sleep, God woke me up and instructed me to read my Bible. It was open to Psalm 34:22 (NKJV): "The Lord redeemeth the soul of his servants, and none of those who trust in him shall be condemned." I was intrigued by those words; it uplifted my soul to know that all I need to do is keep my trust in him. God will redeem his servants over and over again, and take them out of their distress. He knows what we deal with on a day-to-day basis, even when we are the cause of our mishaps. It frightens me to think about what happens to those who don't put their trust in him. God wants to trust you, whoever you are. It doesn't matter where you have been; just remember there are guidelines to follow. Once you put your life in his hands, what is in the dark will come to the light. God has redeemed my soul so many times, I can't count them on a calculator. He wants his people to take control of their lives and live life more abundantly. Loving materials things is not the answer. He gave us dominion over everything on the earth, which should reinforce our joy, but it includes many things that may entice and entrap us in order to deter us as well.

On June 6, 2002, I felt distraught about my life; it seemed as though I would never see light again due to the problems I was facing. I was lying in my bed and had the urge to play basketball, something I love doing very much. But my problems had kept me away from that activity on several occasions in the past. At times in our lives we have to make ourselves get up and do the things we enjoy. This was just one of those times. I took control and did not allow my situation to take my joy. My roommate told me I could ride his bike to the park, and I was glad to leave the house.

When I got to the park, no one was playing ball yet. I decided to ride around until someone showed up to play. I felt like a prisoner who had been released from jail. I saw a nice-looking young lady sitting all alone on a bench. I rode by her a few times, wondering whether I should strike up a conversation with her. Finally, I asked if we could talk. At first, she didn't want to be bothered, but she agreed to talk anyway. I could see that she was dealing with some things as well. I told her it felt good to have a conversation with her about life. I even made her smile, and that made me feel good. We sat and talked about many different topics, including about to whom we should talk to when we needed to be comforted. How else will we grow in the body of Christ if we don't converse with each other? And there are some people you can't talk to about certain things.

Then something strange happened. We saw a three-year-old Latino child wandering around by himself. At first, I didn't think anything about it, but then he cried out for his father. He did not know where his parents were. One part of my mind told not to interfere, because someone might have thought I was trying to abduct the child. My heart suffered to see this baby walking around, crying out for his folks; after that I didn't care what anyone thought. I walked around with this child in my arms, asking some Latino guys if they knew who the father was. They replied no. I also asked two white guys, and they too had no idea. One asked if I wanted to use his phone to call the police. I told him yes because I had been looking for the father for some time and thought I had no other choice. But as the phone began to ring on the other end, his friend walked up and said, "Don't call the police. If the police come, they will take the child." I was frustrated with the parents for letting a three-year-old out of their sight. Nothing is more important than your child, whether you are at a park or anywhere else, as far as I am concerned.

I couldn't bring myself to call the police, because I didn't want to see this child taken away from his parents. The two white guys were also asking around. Not long afterward, a man walked up and said the boy was his child. I was glad we could bring the two back together. I thanked God for helping me make the right choice. If I hadn't been there at that time, it was a great possibility that this baby could have wandered off into the woods. Although it didn't take no more than thirty minutes or so to find the father, that was too long for any child to be wandering alone. This is one of the reasons some of our kids do what they want, because we value something else more than we value them. I don't mean every parent, just the ones who think of their kids as objects. Kids will not always do the right thing, and some may do worse things than others, but we still need to be there for them. The day will come when they really understand what life is about. A new generation has arrived and we must learn new ways to direct them on the right path. Never stop doing the things you enjoy doing, because you may save someone else's life. That day, I helped someone else, and God redeemed my soul.

Never give up on the young; pull back, but never give up on them. In time, hopefully they will get the message. One Saturday my nephew and I went to a sports bar to watch a boxing match; Holyfield was the champion, and Tyson was the contender. In the beginning, everything went well. But at the end of the fight, two gentlemen in the bar started fighting. My nephew was obsessed with fighting. Instead of walking out the door, he walked closer to the two guys who were fighting. To make matters worse, he just had to put his two cents in. One guy pushed a table and accidentally hit my nephew, who was standing too close. That made him mad, and he took off his shirt, ready to fight. God said the battle is not ours, but sometimes we make our own battles. Someone called the police, but before they arrived, my nephew started arguing with one of the security guards. Suddenly the cops showed up, and the staff pointed my nephew out to the police. I couldn't believe what a crazy night this had turned out to be. I knew how wild my nephew can be. We could have walked out the door without any trouble. Instead the police walked my nephew outside and questioned him about this fight. The officer spoke in a quiet toned voice until the manager told the officer that my nephew had run out on a bill and then lied to the police. That really made the officer angry. I sat there, shaking my head. Initially, the officer had asked if I were involved and the manager told him no. I was very upset with my nephew that night, but not to the point where I didn't want to talk to him again. One scripture came to mind: "If you are willing and obedient, you shall eat the good of the land" (Isaiah 1:19 NKJV). If we are willing to do the right things, we shall be successful.

When you work for God, you never know where he may send you, but it is okay to ask why he sent you there. After landing the job with Panasonic, I wondered why I'd been put on night shift, although it didn't matter what shift I was on. My purpose for being there seemed unexplainable, because they'd informed me that I would start on the first shift. I knew that in time God would reveal this secret and the answer to the questioning thoughts would appear. One of my coworkers on night shift was named Moe, who was pretty cool. Our friendship grew as we talked about personal things that we'd both been through in life. I told him I was a minister, not realizing that he was looking for counseling. I told him some awesome things about God; I guess that's what caught his attention, the fact that I was real and passionate about the Word of God. Moe told me that he and a friend had gone out one weekend, and both of them had been drinking and smoking weed. Unfortunately, they had no designated driver, and Moe was driving. After he dropped his friend off, the police stopped him and asked for his identification. As he was reaching into his back pocket to retrieve his wallet, he realized that his gun was under his leg. According to Moe, one of the officers noticed the gun, but didn't say one word. He did notice the empty liquor bottles. Moe said the bottles belonged to his friend, and he'd forgotten to take them out. He had two good things going for him that night: one was that the bottles were empty, and the other was they didn't give him a Breathalyzer test to see if he was intoxicated.

I was overwhelmed by Moe's story because I knew God wanted me to share some knowledge with this eager young man. I told him that God kept him from going to jail and getting a DUI that night. There was no other explanation for his escape; he had been between a rock and a hard place. It seemed as though he had magic like the great Houdini, who created an illusion to escaping death. I also said, "God wanted you to know that he spared your life that night by allowing you to be untouched. He wanted you to seek his love." If someone does something dramatic for you, don't run from them, run toward them. "Behold, I give you the authority to trample on serpents and scorpions, and over all the power of the enemy, and nothing shall by any means hurt you" (Luke 10:19 NKJV). Most of the time, we are our own enemy, which stops us from doing the right things. God has given power to all people, not just preachers, bishops, and deacons, but whoever is willing to worship him in spirit and truth and realize that they must come to a mature level to understand many things. Stop all the nonsense that creates strife for you and for others. Cut out all the lying and backstabbing. You have a choice, just as Moe did, to believe that God has made an escape route. What would you do if this happened to you? Would you draw closer to God?

# CHAPTER 3

# Twin Narra Tree

In some cases, two individuals can make a situation easier than it would have been with only one person. One day I was lying in bed, meditating on God and how wonderful he is to people who love him and to those who don't even believe that he exists. That day I was thinking about a seesaw, and God's words came to me like an overflowing river. When you were a child, did you ever sit on a seesaw, wanting to go up and down, but there was no one else around to split the work with you. It must have been a drag; I know I've been there. Without someone else on the other end of the seesaw, it is impossible to enjoy the ride. You may be willing to go at it alone, but God didn't intend us to take on difficult tasks by ourselves. Instead he is waiting for us to get on the other end so that he can take us higher than we have ever gone before. If we happen to go low, he will pick us up again and again. God revealed his thoughts to me because I stay on the seesaw whether or not there is motion. Many people get on for a while and then jump off when adversity arises. Trouble takes place in all our lives; what else causes us to do what is right? It's unlikely that you'll be able to find this out on your own. Endure the ride of the seesaw, and let it take you to that place where man can't.

Have the heart to help others; you never know when you might need help yourself. My brother and I were leaving our hometown and heading back to Atlanta. Before we got on the road, we stopped at a gas station to fill up. An elderly woman asked my brother if he had some change. He said he didn't, which I knew was not true; he could have spared at least seventy-five cents if he'd wanted to. She asked me the same thing. I told her that all the money I had was going into my car, but I spared one dollar just for her. When I gave it to her, she said thank you, and I told her to thank God, because he laid it on my heart to give her my last. My brother asked if I knew that woman. I told him I didn't have to know her just to give her a dollar. God sends an angel from time to time to test us, to see if our hearts are in the right place, and to see if we are willing to sacrifice for others, as his son Jesus Christ, who laid down his life for us.

Something else happened later on that day that made this story more interesting. When we arrived in Atlanta, close to home, my brother decided to stop and get a sandwich at a convenience store. We walked to the cashier, and he was short one dollar. He told the cashier he needed to get some money from the ATM, and I walked out the door to my car. On the way, I passed a biker who looked like a rebel; I felt that he and my brother might have some encounter. Sure enough, when my brother came out of the store, he said that the biker had given him the dollar he needed to pay for his items. And then my brother said God meant for him to see that. And I agreed, saying, "It was God who wanted you to open up your eyes." My brother had wondered what the old woman would do with any change he gave her. When God puts it on our heart to give, we can't worry about what the person will do with the money. Only God knows, and that's all that matters. Imagine if God were heartless like we are at times and gave based on how he felt about us. We would never understand the true meaning of love.

When I am being led by the spirit of God, I try to write exactly what he lays on my heart. Nevertheless, I am always in an expectant mode. And I believe this was one of those moments. One night on the job, we didn't have enough work to last until the end of our shift. The manager asked a few people if they wanted to go home early. Two guys left at 9:00 p.m., and the rest of us took a break. After break, we always had to check in with the supervisors, who would let us know what needed to be done next. After this break, I walked into the office, but the supervisor asked if I wanted to go home early. I wasn't ready to go yet, because I was enjoying the fact that I was at work and making easy money. My flesh wanted me to stay and make the money, but the answer that came out was from the spirit within me, and it said to leave. When I got into my car, John 4:24 (NKJV) came to mind: "God is a spirit, and those who worship him must worship in spirit and truth." I believed that God, in his true spirit, was advising me to go home. There was something he wanted me to do when I got there. As I opened the door and walked into my home, I heard the phone ringing. It was Jerry, one of the members from my church, who said that they had been trying to reach me all week. If I'd have stayed at work, he would not have reached me. I did not have an answering machine, so he had no way of leaving me a message. I didn't have a cell phone either. Jerry and I were meant to make contact. I know this because I usually got in from work around 11:50 p.m., and he called around 10:00 p.m.—the same time I walked into my door. That was no coincidence!

His reason for calling was related to an incident that had taken place one Sunday before everyone went into church. He didn't understand why things happened the way they did. The piano player had been late for choir practice, although he'd warned the kids not to be late. While Jerry, another man, and I were standing in front of the entrance, the piano player pulled up in his car. Jerry told the piano player that since he wanted the kids to be on time, he needed to do the same. A married couple was going inside the church, and they didn't like what Jerry said to the piano player. Suddenly a bitter quarrel erupted. Jerry couldn't understand why the couple was upset about what he said. I agreed that he was right to tell the piano player that if he wanted the kids to be on time, he definitely needed to be there as well. But I also believe Jerry went about it the wrong way. Over the phone, I said he could have pulled this guy to the side and then voiced his opinion. Sometimes we want someone else to agree with how we view things so that we can get the satisfaction that we are in the right.

As people of God, we have to understand that we must change in so many different ways; our minds can't take it all in at once. We certainly can't accept these changes overnight. God will not give us what our hearts desire if we are not willing to change the way we do things. After I finished speaking with Jerry, I read a scripture that is suited for everyone who thinks it is okay to serve God the same way as they were in the world: "Because I was not cut off from the presence of darkness, and he did not hide deep darkness from my face" (Job 23:17 NKJV). The argument between Jerry, the piano player, and the married couple came back to me after I read this passage. Job seems to be saying that just because we are believers doesn't mean that we will never see darkness again. This darkness can mean an inability to understand the consequences our own actions. But Job is also referring to a dark place where there is no order and anyone can be accused of a crime. As believers, we are not exempt from either type of unpleasant darkness. But they are the avenues that God uses for people to search for his light.

One day God revealed to me that some people can see when he is trying to influence them to follow him and want to take it into consideration, but they either can't or do not want to see how Satan is pulling their strings. How can you see Satan's tricky ways if you don't allow God to show them to you? One of my former coworkers told me he needed to go to church. I told him that it was bad when you know you need to go to church but won't, for whatever reason. That is one of Satan's ways of hiding the truth that God has placed in us. And Satan's job is to keep you from this truth by any means. As soon as you think about going to church, something else enters your mind and tells you that it is more important. At some point in our lives we all take care of something we feel is important, whether someone else says it is good or bad. In any case, we feel that if we don't handle our business on this important thing, there will be consequences. And most of the time, there are! I want to take a situation that many people refuse to accept, myself included, and show you that if you understand the method, you can be free from those unnecessary consequences. A drug dealer who sells drugs for someone else knows that if his mind is not in the right place and he screws up the supplier's money or drugs something bad will happen to him. In some cases, it may not be the drug dealer's fault, but he gets the blame for it. That is why we must take care of those things that pertain to God. When you mess up with man, his trust in you runs out, but God's trust never fades away. In fact, we are the ones who disappear. I am no different. I am also a victim of the outlandish delusions, thinking that my way is the best way. Many times, I needed to take care of those essential things, but I wasn't aware that I was not in total control, even after I did what I shouldn't have. My nephew told me he'd left some weed in his room. I really wanted to smoke it. But I knew if I did, I would have a problem getting it out of my system, and I needed to be clean in case someone called me to work. The unwanted consequences have helped me focus on the important things related to God and not on what I feel is important. We do need to be honest with God, regardless of how much we have grown in his amazing love. Don't be ignorant when God comes into your life with the law of the land.

Don't you hate when a person who knows you are a Christian says a curse word in your presence and then apologizes? I can't understand that whole concept. He is not giving you respect for who you are representing. Why doesn't he take it further and apologize to God? Maybe God will give him new words that will benefit and inspire others. In fact, he is not the first to do such things; a man of God has either been down or is still struggling on that path. It is easier for us to respect man because we react to what we see. But it is better to respect the One who we don't see; in return, we will learn to respect each other even more. God's respect for his people is not marked by favoritism. He doesn't care who you are; his love is great and ready to be shared with many. "That which is already been, and what is to be has already been; and God requires an account of what is past" (Ecclesiastes 3:15 NKJV). Everything that has happened in the past is happening now, and everything that will take place in the future has already happened. For example, people in the past had no respect for God; the same is true today. They heard the Word of God but didn't believe. Some people who say they know God will stab you in the back. Many who say they are your friends end up being your worst enemies. One minute they are smiling in your face, because they enjoy whatever you are doing for them. But once the favor stops, you become their prey.

When I was in the army, I thought that I'd become friends with a pretty cool guy. Hill and I would ride around town for hours, and not one time did I ask him for money for gas. I was just that type of guy and still am today. Hill had no problem telling me when someone else said something about me, so I gave him some credit. There were times when I would leave Sykes's house late, another friend of mine, and pick up Hill from the barracks. Sykes was the type of guy who didn't want you at his house if he didn't know you that well. I'd known Sykes since we were in basic training. I never thought Hill would be a deceptive person, but let me tell the story. One day when Hill and I were driving together, it was raining hard, and I had a wreck. My car was damaged pretty badly, and I couldn't drive it at all. A few months after that, I noticed that Hill had a new friend, which was cool with me, but I didn't expect him to forget about his old friend. I even found out that he'd acquired his own transportation.

Several months passed. Hill and I were no longer friends far as I was concerned, although maybe once in a while we would cross paths and speak to one another. By then I had moved out of the barracks and had no means of transportation. I assumed Hill might ask me if I needed a ride, but that never happened. Despite all the times he rode with me free of charge, he didn't have the decency to ask me one time if there was any place I needed to go. One time I needed a ride but did not ask him. But the day came when he did offer, and I was surprised. I accepted his offer, because I had to go to the store and get a money order to pay a bill. When we returned to my house, he stayed only long enough for me to get out of the car before he pulled off. As he began backing up and heading to the main road, I realized that I'd left my money order in Hill's car. My first thought was to try to wave him down, but I didn't feel like running behind his car to get his attention. So, because I knew him, I thought he would call me or bring it back once he noticed that it was still in his car. Man, was I wrong!

When I got the chance to ask Hill about it, he said he'd mailed it for me, because it was already stamped and ready to go. I said okay, but several days later, a rep from the gas company called to say they had not received my payment. I told them they were wrong because it had been mailed. I trusted Hill had told me the truth. I didn't want to believe that this person who claimed to be a friend had stooped that low. But the unknown slapped me in the face, and I realized that everyone says he is your friend, but it doesn't take but a second to become an enemy. "Faithful are the wounds of a friend; but the kisses of an enemy are deceitful" (Proverbs 27:6 KJV). An enemy can hurt you many different ways, but a friend can wound you by being unfaithful. I was a faithful friend to Hill, even after he stole from me. The wound Hill gave made me see him differently. And it crossed my mind several times to take an eye for an eye approach, especially one day when the opportunity sprung up like a well that had been dry for so long.

I was sitting alone in front of the battalion building. Hill's car was the only one in the parking lot as though it was destiny for me to have my revenge. It was a holiday, and there were hardly any soldiers around. I thought about smashing his windows with a brick, stealing his radio, and flattening all his tires. All these things went through my mind, but I knew they were a setup. And the choice I made then made me the man I am today. I didn't allow revenge to consume me. What would I have proved just to have satisfaction? Love is more than just a four-letter word, and it shouldn't be taken for granted.

Sometimes we mistake lust for love. I thought I was in love with a certain woman, but instead lust clouded my mind and painted a picture of love. Well, this woman popped back into my life after I left the army and moved to Atlanta. She arrived uninvited; I asked her, "What if I had a girlfriend?" Her response was "You'd have to deal with that yourself." I must explain more about this lady so that you can better understand my views. While I was stationed at Fort Bragg, my cousin Alvin introduced me to a sexy lady named Lisa. She had a voluptuous body and was very pretty. At first, she played hard to get, but I didn't care, I was determined to get into her mix. And I thought she might be the one with whom I would settle down. She had it all—body, looks, everything I wanted in a woman. Back then, I was a little blind about everything else, but I soon learned that everything that looks good isn't necessarily good. As time went on, Lisa and I saw more of each other. She'd page me like crazy, and it made me suspect that she wanted to be with me. But it was only bait to reel me into her web, which I didn't realize until after Lisa caught me on her hook. Let me explain: after Lisa and I had sex the first time, I assumed this woman would be mine. I thought I would capture her in the compounds of my fortress; boy, were my thoughts about women rudimentary. My cousin told me to "get it and move on." I suspect he knew something, but he didn't explain why he made that statement. Later, I learned that he used to date Lisa's mother, and the apple doesn't fall too far from the tree.

Once Lisa lured me into her trap, and I had no way of escape, she could move about freely without wondering if I would be there for her. And I was, because she had me where she wanted me. Lisa did things I had never seen before. One time she invited me to dinner. When I arrived at her home, another guy was already there. I suspected that she'd had sex with this guy because there was a hickey on her neck. I was burning up inside, but what could I do? We hadn't agreed that we were in a relationship. In any case, by then my head wasn't attached to my body. I wasn't sure what my mind wanted to do, but my flesh wanted to control everything. I felt like an instrument that she could play however and whenever she wanted.

The next time I faced her, I felt tortured. I was going away for at least two or three months, training in a foreign country, Kuwait. Lisa wanted to see me before I left. The reason why it didn't concern me that much, I was just glad that I would be in her presence. And I wanted to get there by any means necessary. I was hoping the visit would lead to sex, and when I tell you that the sex was the bomb, believe me. I jumped into my car and sped down the highway like a bat out of hell, even though I had finished off two beers and was working on the third one. My license had been suspended, and my tags were expired. I was messed up, but it didn't stop me from going to what I thought was a gold mine.

Not long after I left the house, I went around a curve, following another car. A police car clocked both cars and pulled us over. After the police officer gave the other driver his ticket, he came to my car and asked how much I'd been drinking. I told him the truth. He put me in the back of his squad car and took me back within the city limits, where my cousin lived. Otherwise there's no telling how long I would have been in jail, because they allowed my cousin to put up his house to bail me out, and this was a small town, so everyone knew everyone. I had to pay a $1,300 bond upon my return from Kuwait.

That is not the end of this story. I was determined to see Lisa before I left the United States. When I got out of jail, I called my friend Oreal and asked him to pick me up and take me to see Lisa. But when Oreal dropped me off at Lisa's house, I saw a truck sitting out front. I knocked on the door. Lisa opened it and let me in. I found out the truck belonged to the guy sitting in her kitchen. I said to myself, *This woman must be crazy.* But I was the one who was crazy because I'd taken all this crap from this woman. She spent more time in the kitchen with the other man than she did with me, but I was stuck because I didn't want to ask my friend to come and pick me up so soon. Then Lisa did something I thought was just lowdown and dirty. She went out with this guy and left her two daughters in the house with me. I knew then that I meant nothing to her and neither did her kids. She would do what she wanted to do, no matter what. For all she knew, I could have been a child molester! After all, we'd only known each other for about four or five months.

That will give you a sense of the type of woman I was dealing with; now I can get back to my initial story, about her showing up at my house without my consent. Lisa and I had kept in touch, calling each other from time to time, but I did most of the calling. She'd once resided in Atlanta, but moved back to Saint Paul, North Carolina, to live with her mother because she was facing some hard times and needed help with her newborn. She knew exactly where I lived. But I thought she wanted more between us, so when she surprised me by showing up, that was what I hoped for. I'd had a girlfriend, but she and I had broken up before that day. Meanwhile, I was very glad to see Lisa but also a bit confused. It had been several years since I'd seen her; maybe she knew that she still had her fangs in me. Right away, I asked if she wanted to take a trip with me the following week; we could visit her mother. I didn't foresee any problems, because she was happy to go. When the day came for us to get together, I was very excited. I really thought it was the beginning of something new. I picked up Lisa and her two kids, and we got on the interstate. I told Lisa that our first stop would be my sister's house. We arrived, went in, and sat for about thirty minutes. Then Lisa asked if I were ready yet. The BS had already started, and I knew that more would soon come. Given the lust I had for her, which I thought was love, I felt like I was doing the right thing by saying, "Yes, I am ready," but I really wasn't.

When we arrived at her mother's house, Lisa felt comfortable and started spewing out venom as she'd always done. Her mother had a few visitors. A younger guy about Lisa's age was her mother's roommate; in fact, he and Lisa knew each other from the neighborhood. When she introduced me, I foretold the future; I knew that something would go down with them that night. The older gentleman was her mother's boyfriend; he was very talkative and that was cool with me because it kept my mind off Lisa. She completely ignored me the entire time except when she asked if I wanted something to eat. And once she sat by me for ten seconds to ease my discomfort, which lasted until I dropped Lisa back at her front door. I vowed I would never see that woman ever again.

Let me explain why. As the night wound down, I got very sleepy. Lisa's mom said I could sleep in her older granddaughter's former room. Meanwhile, Lisa and the roommate had gone outside from the backdoor. I had wondered where she would sleep because her mother's roommate had Lisa's old room. I had no idea that it would go down the way it did, because I thought she had some respect for me. I fooled no one but myself.

Lisa and the roommate were drinking; heck, they'd known one another for many years. About three in the morning I decided to lie down, although I didn't want to, because I was wondering where Lisa would sleep; my only concerns were Lisa and my feelings. And, boy, she could affect them in the most unusual way. When I had lied down, I couldn't sleep because I was upset that she had spent so little time with me earlier that day and the night was pretty much over, but not for Lisa and that guy. I was so tired, and I had no choice but to fall asleep. Lisa's daughters slept in their grandmother's room, and the grandmother slept on the couch. I left the door cracked just to see what would happen. I knew Lisa and the guy would come into the house before daybreak. I dozed off for a while, woke up to use the bathroom, and fell right back to sleep, without wondering where Lisa was. I knew that she was up to no good! I was sure that I pulled the door shut. I no longer cared what she did. But it was one of those doors where the hinges are loose, and you can't be positively sure if it is closed all the way after you shut it.

When I woke up, I noticed that my bedroom door was cracked open. I believe God wanted me to see that Lisa was not the woman for me. It didn't matter if the love I had for her grew like a vine tree, she was a very frivolous woman, never serious. It didn't it matter to her if my heart was being deceived. I didn't matter to her in any way. I saw Lisa come out from the roommate's room and walk into the bathroom. I thought that maybe the roommate had stayed at a friend's house, but after a minute he followed right behind her. God was showing me what I would get myself into if I kept cultivating this lust, although it felt very much like love.

In the morning I left the house for a while, because I thought I'd been betrayed; my blood was boiling like lava. When I came back inside, I told Lisa I was ready to leave. She just sat there. I told her about four times that I was ready, and yet she still didn't move. I got so mad that I just sat in the car and waited for her. When it came to Lisa, there were no rules. I was like a feather blowing in the wind. When she finally came out, I had been sitting there for about an hour. Even though this situation was miserable, it was also a blessing, because it helped me come to my senses. Christians know that God uses adversity to make us take routes that are different from the ones we are currently traveling. For our own protection, we must maintain our relationship with God even through confusion; that is the only way we can discern right from wrong. "You shall love the Lord your God with all your heart, with all your soul, and with all your might" (Deuteronomy 6:5 NKJV). Why that is so hard to understand? If we learn how to love, then everything else we do will be less painful. We need to stop acting as though we created ourselves. "For if anyone is a hearer of the word and not a doer, he is like a man observing his natural face in a mirror" (James 1:23 NKJV). Whenever you look into a mirror, ask yourself, "Can I see God, who formed me into existence? Or am I just a man who seeks his own heart?" In life, we may not get everything that we want, but having love is the icing on the cake. "And now abide faith, hope, love, these three; but the greatest of these is love" (1 Corinthians 13:13 NKJV). Don't mistake lust for love. I'd thought that I loved Lisa with my heart, but that love was overpowered by lust. Real love occurs when you are willing to bridge the gap between you and someone else.

If there is a way to bridge the gap between you and someone else, especially a family member, then take action. Rectify the problem, if possible, because you won't have many chances to show them your love. For example, once I was sitting at work and thinking about an awful thing I'd done to one of my sisters. I'd asked her to cosign on a loan for me through a finance company she'd dealt with for years. I would have done it myself, but my credit was shot to death. She actually cosigned three loans. I paid back the first and the second, but with the third, I lost sight, specifically, I lost my job by being ignorant, not caring about anyone else but myself. Once I realized the mistake I had made, I was disappointed with myself. My sister said she would take me to court, because I'd left her with this bill. She probably wasn't serious; maybe she wanted to scare me a bit so that I would pay back the loan. But the fact that she told me such a thing meant that things were not good between us, and she had the right to say it. Whether or not she meant it, the words had been exposed in the air. I got to the point where I didn't want to call her, because my words didn't equal my actions. I wondered if she realized this incident had hurt me as much as it hurt her. I knew I was a better man than that; I was just young and foolish.

I knew my sister no longer trusted me. I hoped that one day God would make a way for me to correct this mistake and return us to a place where trust reigned again. I wanted to pay her back all the money I owed her and then help her out as much as I could, because I felt obligated. With time, I made that happen, because my actions spoke louder than my words. Actions always speak louder than words, and they can be used to bridge gaps, regain trust, growing your business, etc. We shouldn't allow anything to get in the way of loving our siblings or friends. Sometimes it may seem as though that is impossible. I have issues with some of my siblings, but I hope and pray that one day that will no longer be true. You never know when you may need the help of others, so bridge any gap that you can.

One time I was worrying that my check would be garnisheed for child support. I prayed and asked God to help me out. The problem seemed too much for me to handle. But I also had to dig deep and tell myself that God would take care of it. I called the Child Support Services Division and gave them the information about my employment. I didn't want to, but I had to because I wasn't making that much money anyway. For God to hear us and to move on our behalf, we might have to do things we don't want to do. The next day I went to work, and in the evening, my supervisor asked if I wanted to come in early the next morning, so I could make some overtime (and thus pay my child support). "Ask, and it will be given to you; seek, and you will find; knock, and it will be opened to you" (Matthew 7:7 NKJV).

Before asking about anything else, first ask God to help us seek his face, because nothing else really matters. Think about it for a moment; you will leave everything you have behind after you leave this world. It would be a sad thing to gain the whole world but lose your soul once you leave it. If you knock on the door the right way, God will open it. God will give us what we want, but it may not be exactly how we pictured it. Sometimes we say, "If he doesn't give it to me exactly as I want it, then he is not giving me what I want." But God weighs and knows the heart of a man. Abrasiveness keeps us sharp. What doesn't kill a person only makes him stronger.

After God blesses us, he doesn't want us to turn our backs on him. Sometimes a person will say, "If God blesses me with that, then I will do this in return." As soon as God does his part, the person forgets that God had any part in it. It becomes a cycle; we don't know when to stop and be men of our word.

"A prudent man foreseeth the evil, and hideth himself: but the simple pass on, and are punished" (Proverbs 22:3 KJV). Many times when we do stupid things and then we get in trouble as a result, we believe God is punishing us. But the truth is that God will remain true to his word. I met a woman who lived in my apartment complex. I wanted to get to know her and asked her to dinner. After awhile I realized she was married, which made me leave her alone. One day, I met her husband and chatted with him for a while. Months passed, and I stopped seeing them around the complex; I figured they'd moved but wasn't sure. Another day I ran into her husband, and he told me they had indeed moved. But then I saw his wife at the car wash. I wanted to approach her, but there was a guy next to her drying his car off; I thought he might be her boyfriend. I kept my distance even though I wanted to say hello. I got in my car and had almost reached the main road, when the guy pulled off. That gave me the opportunity to go back and speak with her, because I'd heard that her marriage wasn't doing so well. That might seem selfish, but one man's trash is another man's treasure. Maybe she'd gotten a divorce and was ready to meet someone else. I asked her how her husband was doing. She confirmed that they'd broken up, and I was glad to hear that news. My next question was, "Would you like to go to church with me on Sunday?" I gave her a card with the church's information, and she asked if my personal phone number was on the card as well. If so, she would call. I gave her my home phone number; I thought it could lead to something promising.

I called her the next night around 11:30 p.m., and she told me to call her the following day around 5:30 p.m., because she was tired after work and school. When we did connect, we talked about life and God. I told her I was a minister and about my belief in God. She told me the most upsetting thing, which made me reconsider everything. She and her husband were still living together, and she didn't want me to say anything if I called and her husband picked up the phone. If that happened, I was to hang up the phone and not say a word. I told her I didn't want to play those types of games. She said she felt obligated to stay with the man because they were still married. You should not feel obligated to someone who brings only misery into your life. I don't know what she was going through, and she did not care to tell me. But if your spouse is not willing to go to counseling to improve the marriage, then why should you remain? She also said her husband knew the Bible like the back of his hand. I hope that wasn't a reason she felt obligated to stay with him. Satan knows what the Bible says and doesn't mind using it against people who don't know it for themselves. I could see the evil that was brewing because I was a prudent man.

Sometimes you learn who people are when you talk to them. I'd mentioned to my coworker Edmond that one of the line leaders had seen me fixing a flat tire and walked right by me without offering to help. There is nothing wrong with feeling that people may need your help from time to time. Edmond said that he believed people would help out. And I told him, "They don't care anything about you!" God opened Edmond's eyes and showed him that I was right about this issue. I was on my forklift and picking my orders for the night; one order required me to lift a pallet about two or three feet from the floor and then climb onto the pallet to reach an item. But as I was climbing down, I began losing my balance and was about to fall. To stop my fall, I grabbed onto the rail of the rack with my left hand, and held onto the forklift with my right. As I tried to regain my balance, something popped in my left shoulder blade, and it hurt like hell, whatever hell feels like. The pain was excruciating; I had never experienced anything like it before.

My first thought was to tell my employers and then go home. However, I needed the money. I also didn't think it was that bad, because as quickly as the pain came, it went. At least that's what I thought at first; but when I moved it a certain way, the pain would return. I thought I'd dislocated it but wasn't sure. Edmond said I should tell the assistant manager so he could write a report. I took his advice. After some time had passed, the assistant manager told the supervisor to check on me to see if I was all right. The supervisor sent a coworker.

I painted this picture with words for Edmond, who thought about what I'd described. He said I was right, that he had experienced something similar that proved to him that the managers didn't care. God allows things to happen to one person so another person can see more clearly and gain more knowledge. I thank God for using me as his stunt double so that others might be protected. As children of God, we must remain on guard every day, because we never know when our help will be needed. I've said it before, and I'll say it again, but I am inviting you to drink from an ancient chalice that has more knowledge on history than any man. If only it had ears and a voice, it could tell us how everything connects one way or another. Even to a woman having a dream about her son, it still passes through time and becomes a part of history.

The next day, one of the security guards, Willie, told me that another guard, Will, had passed out and was in the hospital. I didn't think it was too serious because Will was supposed to return to work the following day. I found out from Will that I didn't get the whole story. Will had been foaming from the mouth. The day he passed out, his mother had a dream about a man who had a white cloud over his head; his hand was around his neck, and he was grasping for air. He said the dream scared his mother. He asked me what I thought it meant. At first I thought it was about him, but after pondering on it I decided that it was intended for her. Let me explain why. Will said his mother loved him more than she loved her other children; in addition, she hadn't been living right. I told him that God was trying to show his mother that if she didn't get her life in order, he would take from her the very person she loved most.

You might think that God will abandon people who do not live right, but in some cases he may take away someone you love. Maybe that will help the person who isn't striving to live right to see that they shouldn't take life for granted; why throw it away for a stupid reason? God wants to save as many souls as he can. Of course, we humans don't like the way God gets his points across. I have learned how to appreciate and embrace those signs of God. Stop means stop, and anyone who disagrees really needs help. God is amazing when it comes to the people who love him. Remember the incident in which I hurt my shoulder? When I went to work the next day, I wondered how I would pull orders when I could barely move my arm. I knew that I wasn't fit to lift anything. I checked in with my supervisor, who just issued the orders. Not once throughout the whole night did I have an order in which I had to use my arm. I never imagined that God would bless me in that particular way. That may sound corny, but it is the truth. At first, I didn't realize it was a blessing, but later on I knew in my heart that it was. I had to be blind not to see it as so.

When is it time to repent for your sins and turn from your wicked ways? When it is too late? God sometimes keeps us in a bad situation and uses that situation to change a man's life for the better or to open his eyes so he can see there is a higher power. Only God can alter a person's thought process. I went over to a friend's house. An older gentleman was there; he'd been drinking for a while. He asked me to take him to the store. I was happy to give him a ride. The drink must have loosened him up a bit, because on the way he said he had something heavy to lay on me. This could have been because I'd told him I was a minister. He said a good while back he'd bought some drugs for himself and a woman. After they had smoked the drugs, he wanted to have sex with the woman, but she said no because she was a lesbian. That put him in such a rage, he got a shotgun, loaded it, and demanded that she open her mouth. He placed the gun into her mouth and pulled the trigger, but the gun did not fire. For years, he didn't understand why things happened the way they did, but he was thankful that God kept his gun from firing. At the same time, he wondered why he found it so hard to get a job. In addition, he didn't have any money in his pocket and he was about to get evicted. He asked me, "Where is God now?"

God will alter an individual's life, but after he has done that, the rest is up to us. We have to force ourselves to make better decisions if God is to show favor on his people. Recognizing something is one thing, but learning to appreciate what you have learned is a tool that can help you. You will not appreciate anything if there is no change within you. And when you don't want to change, you have few concerns about anything in life. Your beliefs in God will remain stagnant because you are unwilling to move forward. Gain control over your life; get up and do something.

This guy seemed ready to lose his mind because of the cards he was dealt. The only thing he could do was turn from his ways and trust in God. We are the only ones who know when to hold or fold. We all have chances to change our ways, but the fact remains—changing is up to us. The most reasonable and simplest answer I could give him was to seek God's divine wisdom, understanding, and knowledge. I want to make a point to everyone who believes that drinking, smoking, and doing drugs is a cure: it only takes away your pain for a while. I beg you to wake up from that nightmare and allow God to bring you into reality with confidence.

Many people who smoke cigarettes believe they can't function without them, but let me share the news about cigarettes. They are among the deadliest killers in the world. Wouldn't it be nice to have clean lungs once again, not to spend most of the time coughing, or to be able to run like you used to do? I used to smoke cigarettes like they were going out of style; I was not a chain smoker, but I could put them away. I had to find a way to stop smoking because my throat began to hurt. And that outlet came for me when I saw the strong hold they had on someone else. At work one day, I heard a female coworker coughing so bad, I thought she would cough up her lungs. I wondered what caused her to cough like that. She told me that her doctor said she couldn't stop smoking cigarettes until after she had an operation. I'd imagined it would be the other way around, but those cigarettes have a way of throwing you for a loop. It's sad, but this woman's tragic illness helped me to incinerate my urge for smoking, because I didn't want to be in her position. I must warn you: if you try to quit, Satan is real, and he will tempt you the best way he knows how. Not long after I quit, I walked outside of my apartment. I didn't go far. I stayed in the walkway and just happened to look down; there was a box of Newports in front of me. They were my favorite cigarettes. When I opened the top of the box with my foot, it was almost half full. I picked the box up and my first thought was to smoke one. I had many things on my mind, and they were stressing me out. Instead, I got enough courage to crush the box and throw it in the trash, because I knew that cigarettes would not solve my problems but only make my life more complicated.

"Therefore submit to God, resist the devil and he will flee from you" (James 4:7 NKJV). One way you can resist the devil is by not falling for his enticements. However, I must tell you the truth: there are some things that we will do. If you do give in and are consumed by indulgence, the problem still will be there and you will not feel any different. Keep the body healthy as much as possible, and you will be able to maintain your way of living on many levels. If I just do what God expects of me, then the devil will flee for a while. But he always comes back in a different form or fashion. God wants his people to be strong when they are being tempted by the devil. Look at other smokers and take note of their condition; maybe that will give you some strength to quit. Some people are overwhelmed by the tar and nicotine of cigarettes.

I had another encounter with a lady who smoked cigarettes. I met her as I was walking back from the store. I mentioned how bad cigarettes were, and she said if she stopped smoking today, she could die tomorrow from something else. And she was right; none of us knows the time or hour of our departure from this world. But we don't have to leave as fools either. I wish there was something else I could have said to her to clarify my point. Why would you suffer from something that you might have been able to prevent? For instance, some smokers think they won't ever get cancer, but they end up dying from it. They probably had several family members and friends who tried to get them to stop, but they allowed Satan to play them like a fiddle.

Let us talk about a scripture that might open the mind of a person with a one-track mind. Solomon said, "Moreover I saw under the sun: in the place of judgment, that wickedness was there; and in the place of righteousness, iniquity was there" (Ecclesiastes 3:16 NKJV). You may think people are righteous, but they are just the opposite. Many of these places to which Solomon refers, where both good and evil reside, are references to corrupt people who camouflage themselves as good. I hope the following stories will make you step back for a moment and see the truth.

The first incident is about a friend of mine who had a run-in with the police. One night he was going to an ATM, but before he could pull into one of the parking spaces, he saw a policeman staring as if he were nothing. So he stared back. He thought about pulling alongside the cop so he wouldn't seem like a thug or someone looking to commit a crime. But once he opened his door, the policeman told him to turn down his music, which wasn't playing that loudly. My friend leaned into his car and turned down his music; he didn't want to provoke this officer. That is not the end to this story. After he turned down his music, the policeman asked to see his license. That was when my friend got upset, because he knew he had not done anything wrong. My opinion was that the policeman was trying to create a problem when there really wasn't one. My friend also mentioned that the cop was black; maybe he was jealous of his car. Sometimes when people achieve some type of position, they use it to discriminate their own kind. It is a crying shame to know that our so-called protectors are sometimes worse than the criminals. I am not saying that all cops are bad, but if you are supposed to uphold the law, then do it the right way. Policemen have tough jobs, but harassing people for nothing is crazy.

The second incident is about one of the line leaders at one of my previous employers. One day my coworker Terry asked if Mr. Canton, the assistant manager, had informed me that we could come in on Saturday to work. I told Terry no. What made it so bad was that Mr. Canton had walked right by me earlier that day and never said one word about letting me work extra hours. I didn't dwell on it, but I asked the supervisor later on that evening if I could come in as well, just to see what he would say. The supervisor said that Mr. Canton already had the crew he needed. And the crazy thing was that same supervisor asked two other guys if they wanted to work right after my conversation with him. I told my supervisor I felt as though someone had something against me. And, of course, his response was, "It is nothing like that." But I couldn't see it any other way. If one guy didn't want to work, why pass me up and ask someone else? Minutes later, my supervisor and I crossed paths again; he told me it was okay if I came in the next day, and he would take the heat if something were said. When Saturday came, I changed my mind, because I'd had to deal with too much junk in order for them to let me work. It wasn't like I was a bad worker or late for work. I would have handled the situation differently if I had been a leader. Just because people are leaders doesn't mean they know how to lead. Wherever you think righteous is, take a step back, because wickedness could be there as well; most of the time it is. Solomon's eyes could see through the bull crap of man's wicked ways, but the men, with their ordinary eyesight, could not see what life was truly about.

# CHAPTER 4

# Cotton Tree

Dreams can have a significant effect on your life, if you interpret them and put them in perspective. I had an interesting dream one Sunday morning before I went to church. I was stooped down behind an object, scared out of my wits, because arrows were being aimed my way. My father was also in this dream; he was in danger as well, but I wasn't sure of his whereabouts. To save him, I had to stand up and face the arrows. I realized that I couldn't allow fear to stop me from trying to save my father. When I stood up and began looking for my father, I noticed he was behind me and was safe. Even though I had no idea where my father was, I had to sacrifice myself and do what felt right in my heart.

Suddenly, I woke up. I was crying and thinking that I had to save my father. At first, I thought this dream was intended for my father, but that wasn't true because he was no longer living. It was meant for me, because the spirit of fear can keep anyone from advancing in life—spiritually, mentally, physically, and financially, etc. And when I arrived at church that morning, we stood as the pastor read the scripture. I said to myself, "It would be ironic if he began reading from the same page that I am already on." Still, when he said, "Turn your Bibles to Luke 19, verses 1 to 4," I was stunned and astonished, even though I was on that page and looking at that very scripture:

> Then Jesus entered and passed through Jericho. Now behold, there was a man named Zacchaeus, who was a chief tax collector, and he was rich. And he sought to see who Jesus was, but could not because of the crowd, for

he was of short stature. So he ran ahead and climbed up into a sycamore to see him, for he was going to pass that way. (NKJV)

I compared this passage to my dream, and it helped me to understand that I should not be afraid of rising to the top but use the resources that God has given me to get there. I could see how the short tax collector would be afraid to walk in a crowd of taller people. But he couldn't let fear stop him from seeing Jesus. When Jesus saw him, he told him to come down from the tree. I know the tax collector must have felt great joy when Jesus saw him. No matter what you fear, seek Jesus and believe that everything will fall in place according to his will.

Are we so focused on the material things that we can't see reality? Once I was out and about, and I saw a woman I'd known for quite some time. I told her I'd seen her on another day, and she looked nice. She said, "I would look even nicer if I were driving a Mercedes." I hate to sound harsh, but just because you have a nice car doesn't mean that you will look better. It also won't change the way you think. Your attitude could get worse; you may think that you are better than others just because of what you have. If you have a car that takes you from point A to point B, be thankful, because someone else would love to be in your shoes. We all like to have nice things, but it takes work to acquire them. Her belief that a Mercedes would make her look nicer was a childish way of thinking. "When I was a child, I spoke as a child, I understood as a child: but when I became a man, I put away childish things" (1 Corinthians 13:11 NKJV). We must act maturely and stop acting and thinking like children. Having nice things can make someone feel better and can create a sense of pride. At one point, my car made me feel more confident about talking to women. How stupid of me! You don't need anything or anyone to make you feel proud of yourself or realize that you are a good person. Everything we have every wanted will disappear and will mean nothing to us after we have left this place. But God has many riches in heaven, which earthly riches can't compare.

If you give back to God—pay your tithes, support his ministries, or help the less fortunate—you will reap what you sow. I had no problem giving back to the Lord. When I got paid, before I did anything else, I placed my tithe in my Bible and did not touch it until I went to church.

And God gave back to me. One time Dean, a friend of mine, asked me to help his mother move. I told him yes; I was not looking for anything in return, but Dean said he'd give me a hundred dollars anyway. He gave it to me about a week before his mother was to move. When moving day came, Dean's mother asked him if he'd taken care of me. He told her yes. I guess Dean didn't convince her, because then he asked me in front of her. And my response was yes. But when I was listening to them talking I was thinking to myself, *What if his mother tried to offer me something else?* I wasn't sure what I would do if she did. But I did know that I didn't want to take advantage of either one of them. With a smile on her face, she walked over to me and handed me an additional forty dollars, saying, "Here is a tip." I told her no, but she insisted I take it. "Look at it as a blessing from God," she said. I received that blessing because I gave to God, who blesses people who keep his commandments.

Many times, I can't understand or express how I feel about myself, because of the different challenges I face every day. Sometimes I feel so bad, but down inside I feel good and know that God is in control. "Therefore my spirit is overwhelmed within me; my heart within me is distressed" (Psalm 143:4 NKJV). I do feel down and out because I am lonely. I hope one day to meet someone I can trust. I've realized that it isn't good to jump into a situation and not look toward God for guidance. I have fallen short of this goal several times in my life, and after it didn't work, I felt as though I would never be happy again and like my whole world had been turned upside down. If you are optimistic about life and do whatever you want, then you need to understand Proverbs 16:2 (NKJV): "All the ways of a man are pure in his own eyes, but the Lord weighs the spirits." You know the story about Adam and Eve eating the fruit from the tree of good and evil. God asked Adam where he was, and Adam was afraid to answer. Adam knew they had messed up totally. God then asked Adam why he'd eaten from the tree of good and evil after he'd been forbidden to do so. Adam said the woman gave the fruit to him. Eve then blamed it on the serpent.

We need to learn from the past and know that God means what he says. Satan convinced Adam and Even that if they ate from the tree they would be wise like God and have his power. We take many things for granted in order to try to get more than what we already have, without thinking about the aftermath. Adam and Eve had no problem putting the blame on someone else, like people often do in today's world. When will we admit our own wrongdoings? Putting the blame on others does not mean that you have escaped; it just prolongs your punishment. After they ate of the tree of good and evil, God made them see that they were naked and ashamed. God doesn't want us to be ashamed while we are living for his purpose. And when you do things your way, you never know what can happen.

One time I was driving on a suspended license, and I switched the sticker from my motorcycle to my car, trying to beat the system. My brother Willie warned me that I might get caught, but I didn't pay him any attention because I thought I had everything under control. Every time he brought up the matter, I'd quickly change the subject. My brother's warning became a reality. One day I was coming from the tech school, taking the back roads as a precaution. About ten minutes from my apartment complex, I passed a policemen parked on the opposite side of the road. I wasn't driving over the speed limit or doing anything else wrong. Still, I had an eerie feeling. I wanted to stop at the corner store to get something to snack on, but a voice told me to go straight to the house. Instead, I stopped at the store, and while I was in there, the policeman parked outside. I could see him waiting for me to come out. When I stayed in the store longer than he expected, he pulled right behind my car. When I did go out, he said, "You weren't going to come out of the store, were you?" I told him that I was. But I really didn't want to come out, because I knew I was caught. He then asked, "Is this your car?" I couldn't lie, so I told him about my tag, license, and insurance. I was locked up as a result, all because I had not taken my brother's advice seriously. At one time I would have figured that the cop pursued me because I was black and had a nice car with rims. But if that were not the case, then his reason for stopping me was trivial. If we live by God's law, then we are no longer under the law of the land, because God's laws are more satisfying to live by than the law of the land.

One morning I was lying in bed thinking about how our lives are equivalent to traveling through tunnels. I knew that God wanted me to write down that thought, but I didn't do so at that very moment. I went to work and went to clock in. One of the women who worked in the office walked alongside me. I told her about this fifteen-year-old preacher who visited my church and preached a very eloquent, powerful, and inspiring sermon. For some reason, right before the end of our conversation, she said, "There is light on the other side of the tunnel." I hadn't mentioned one word to her about my dream, but her comment created a sense of urgency in me to write about it. Before you travel through a tunnel, there is always light on the other side, whether you see it or not. It is good to believe that it is light; it will ease your mind when you are in a dark place.

When many people get into dark places in their lives, they lose hope that they can reach the light on the other side. The dark frightens them so much they can't think straight, and you have to think clearly to find your way through the dark. Of course, some people need encouragement from others to help them through. They worry that the tunnel will cave in and crush them or that someone else will run them off the road. Many refuse to go through the tunnel at all, because they are too scared.

It is good to go through dark places every now and then. And the only way to see the light is to face the dark. The Bible says that God is the truth, the light, and the way. The remarkable thing is that God uses the dark to empower people to produce the good (i.e., the light that is in us). "For he made him who knew no sin to be sin for us, that we might become the righteousness of God in him" (2 Corinthians 5:21 NKJV). God had Jesus take on man's sin, the darkest place, which no person will ever see. Only God could deal with what he created. We are no match for sin. That's why when we sin, we get out of control and get ourselves in so much trouble. But the experience also can make us wise, if we take the time to learn from it. The wonderful thing about Jesus, who knew no sin, was that he was not worried about being in a place that could blind his vision. He knew what he had to do, because that was his task. The Lord wasn't going to allow sin to prevail over his Son. But without that dark entity, how can anyone be thankful for light? How would you know that light existed if there were no darkness?

The last part of 2 Corinthians 5:21 says "that we might become the righteousness of God." The problem is we choose not to know that we can be made righteous. Don't be afraid to come to the light of God. When I was in the military, I went with a friend to a beach party in Savannah, Georgia. As soon as we parked, this girl walked up toward us with a video camera; she wanted us to take our penises out so she could record them. My friend and I had the same looks on our faces and probably were thinking the same thing: *This girl must be crazy.* There weren't many people around, but if a cop had been there, who knows what we'd have had to deal with. A guy we didn't know walked up, and this girl asked him the same thing she'd asked us. He pulled out his penis in public. I could never do something so irrational. I have done some crazy things, but that was something I just wouldn't do. It is too far out there. This is a good example of why we need God in our lives to direct us toward victory. Don't be a fool for the world. Be a fool for God; it doesn't matter what others think about you. Someone is bound to judge you, so why not let them judge you for being a child of God with dignity, honesty, and truth. I know we can do better; we must strive for perfection. I hear others say all the time: we are not perfect. This is a very true statement, but it doesn't mean we cannot strive to be perfect. Something has to be wrong with a mind that just does things without thinking or caring about the consequences. Dig deeper into your hearts, minds, and souls to find the love that can ease the pain for many people. There are no buts about it; saying but is only an excuse to sin freely with no consequences.

In mid-2002, a coworker and I had a pretty serious conversation about God. While I was doing most of the talking, he seemed interested in the things I was speaking about. I mentioned that I was a minister, and one night he said he had to talk to me about something very important. As we left work and I was headed to my car, he stopped me and told me that something in his past was haunting him. After he'd gotten married, he cheated on his wife, and now she was asking if he'd ever cheated on her. She'd asked him more than a couple of times, and he always answered no.

I told him the heavy burden he was carrying around was the lie he told to her. He said this thing had been on his mind for a long time, and he didn't know what to do. I know many people wouldn't agree with what I told him because society in general thinks it is strange. I said he had to tell her the truth to have a clear vision of this matter and move forward with his marriage, or he'd have to keep dealing with his subconscious that was emitting pain and anguish into his heart.

Whatever you do the truth can be exposed, with or without your consent. I told my coworker that God doesn't like us to keep secrets from the people we love. How can God use you if you do not understand the meaning of love? After a few days passed, my coworker told me he was going to confess to his wife. I guess he wanted to prepare himself for the worst, which is very understandable. I didn't think that he would take my advice and risk losing his wife. The next day, he said, "Man, I did it." He looked distraught; he was afraid his wife would leave him. When I was younger, I didn't have the nerve to tell my wife the truth about a phone number she found, even though I had not had sex with that woman. But when my wife asked me about the number, I told her that it was for a job, knowing damn well I was lying. That mistake allowed me to help someone else make the right choice. I was very proud that my friend rose above his old selfish ways and stood up for himself as a man.

About two days later, after he came clean with his wife, he and I talked about his situation again. But this time I informed him about having blemishes. In the Old Testament, people had to sacrifice a burnt offering unto God for their sins. Whatever that offering was, it had to be without blemishes or spots. They had to give God their best before he would forgive their sins. I guess that must have struck a nerve because my friend said he'd told his wife only part of the truth. I asked, "What do you mean?" She had asked with how many different women he had cheated. I told him, "Well, you know what you have to do. If you had just told her everything the first time, then you wouldn't have anything else to hide and you would not be stressed out." I also wanted him to understand that no matter what happens, God is bigger than his problem. "So don't chase her," I said. "She has to make her own decision." Sometimes doing the right thing will destroy a relationship. But at the same time it will make God smile down on you because you chose to open up and blossom like a flower in the summer, waiting for bees to gather its pollen, which is a wonderful thing. This man was on the verge of losing his wife, but God moved in a mighty way. Several days later, my friend told me that his wife had kissed him and said that she loved him. And months afterward, they had their first child.

God moves in our lives in a special way when we are obedient. My friend shared his story with one of his close friends, and his friend said he'd told his girl that he had cheated on her. And then my friend's wife told her friend, and her friend told her boyfriend what she had done behind his back. I told one person to strive and live a truthful life; he accepted it, and it was like a wild fire that couldn't be tamed.

I learned that it was in my best interests to watch what I say when it came to Satan, because he loves to tap dance and thrives on the music we play. After my friend and I finished our conversation, Satan jumped on something I said; he toyed with me. I told my friend that Satan couldn't mess with me. I felt that I had done something great by giving him some helpful advice, and I thought I was untouchable. I quickly had to revise that opinion, because later on that day two guys walked up to my friend and said they needed to talk with him. One of them was the assistant manager. My friend told me their conversation was about me. I was a bit upset, because they could have talked to me if there were a problem. But since the assistant manager knew my friend a little better than he knew me, he asked my friend if I had pulled the wrong orders. I found that strange because the assistant manager checked the orders after we pull the products. For some odd reason, I believed this manager was trying to get me into trouble. Once he spoke to me about stopping in the aisle and holding a conversation with my friend. But often when I did that, it wasn't like we were in a rush to pull orders, and after the manager talked to me, I had no problem correcting the issue.

The most upsetting and disturbing thing was that the manager called a coworker in his office to inquire about my work ethic. I would have felt better if he had approached me instead. The devil can use a Christian who lacks knowledge of God. I think Satan took my bold statement—that I felt untouchable—and turned it against me by using someone else to agitate me for no reason. But it frightened me a bit, to think I might lose my job. Be careful what you say! That day when I got home, I opened my Bible to Psalm 27:1–4 (NKJV):

> The Lord is my light and my salvation; whom shall I fear? When the wicked came against me to eat up my flesh, my enemies and foes they stumbled and fell. Though an army may encamp against me, my heart shall not fear; though war may rise against me, in this I will be confident. One thing I have desired of the Lord, that I will seek; that I may dwell in the house of the Lord all the days of my life; to behold the beauty of the Lord, and to inquire in his temple.

No matter what tries to bring down your hopes, remember that God is the strength of your life. Retain this knowledge in your heart and when you need it, it will be there to eradicate anything the enemy tries to do. However, if God is to give us this remarkable power, we must seek him first. And also this must be a way of life, because it gives us the stability to deal with the unusual things that appear.

When I went to work the next day, I still had this thing on my mind, about the manager trying to cause a problem. My first instinct was to walk into his office and confront him, but I had to think for a moment and not jump to conclusions. I was thinking that the manager might come and tell me himself about his intention of letting me go, because in the past he'd come directly to me. But I felt like my friend had given me a heads up. Satan is always busy trying to get us to stop doing what is right. That is why you have to look at a situation before assuming that you are right. To smooth things out with the manager, I told him that I would rather be friends than enemies. I didn't care if what he said was true or not. The fact remains I can't be moved by a force that God controls.

A good method is to use your thoughts about being successful to persuade your mind to counteract laziness. And when the urge is there to work, simply act on it. You must be able to gather strength from somewhere to be able to push. Remind yourself that you are the head and not the tail. I was waiting in my car because city workers were repairing the road, and I had a great urge to write. If you have ever driven a car, then you know sometimes it takes awhile to get moving. This was one of those days, and I thought I might sit for at least fifteen minutes. You can't be successful if you don't do anything. Before I could write one sentence, the cars in front of me started pulling forward. I was glad that the traffic was moving, but it also took away that urge to write. I thought about it and decided to write about the incident. It seemed as though a force greater than I had stolen the urge for me to write. But it also made the situation more interesting and gave me a better understand of why things happen. These are only my opinions about how we should view this fictitious world in which we live. Losing that urge can keep you from the finish line, which is where your greatest blessing might lie. The only way you will accomplish what is set before you is to think in a logical way. On one hand, we want to believe that success will fall into our lap, but on the other hand we must acknowledge reality and we must follow certain rules and guidelines. God will always be there to help you, even though it may not seem like it. God has been there for me in the past, even when I thought that he wasn't. It became evident that he was there.

Once my brother Johnny owned a pretty red sports car that was very fast. When he first brought it home, it caught my eye like it was an attractive woman. Johnny said he would let me drive his car to my prom. I was too excited. Two things happened for me, one unfortunate and one fortunate. Well, about two weeks before the prom, my brother wrecked his car; thank God, he didn't get hurt. Unfortunately for me, I wasn't able to drive that pretty red car. The fortunate thing, I didn't find out about until many years later. For a long time, I wondered why this accident had to happen close to my graduation day. As we get older, God allows us to wonder about things in the past and get some answers to those questions. God has a way of keeping us from danger even when we can't see it. Let me explain. I am not glad that my brother wrecked his car, but at the same time I believe it was for a purpose. The night of the prom, my girlfriend and I were riding with two of my high-school friends, Bill and Larry. Two of my other friends who came along had their own cars. The three cars trailed one another after we left Statesboro, Georgia, where we'd gone after the prom to celebrate. Thank God I wasn't driving my brother's sport car, because everyone began racing to see who could get back home first. We were stopped by the police, and they locked up my friends, who were driving eighty-five in a fifty-five miles-per-hour zone. And two of them remained locked up, because they didn't have enough money to pay their way out of jail. Now this is why it was fortunate for me, because if I had been driving my brother's car—and I was a true speed demon—there is no telling what may have happened that night. I didn't come into this knowledge until after many years had passed, but God made it clear that he was with me. He hindered me from being a real speed demon, which may have led me to hell.

God kept me from danger at a different time. I was leaving my sister's home in Wrens, Georgia, and I was going to work in Augusta. The two towns were about forty miles apart; on the way, I picked up a friend. Most of the time, and when we got off from work, I'd go by his house in Augusta to take a nap before driving back home. We both were on that graveyard shift, which makes you feel like you are dead when it is time to clock out. Anyway, on this particular morning, I decided not to take a nap at my friend's house; instead I dropped him off and kept driving. My mind told me that I was all right to drive, but my body indicated something totally different. I listened to my mind, which wasn't the brightest thing to do at that point. After driving on the road for a while, I felt my eyes getting heavier and heavier. I would quickly reopen them when I felt them closing. I even stuck my head out the window, hoping some fresh air would end my fatigue. All of a sudden, I fell into a deep sleep, and when I woke up, I was in a ditch on the other side of the road. I was amazed that no car or truck had been in the other lane, because if there had been, I probably wouldn't be here today. Many of you have been in bad situations and didn't understand why things turned out well. God made sure at that specific time that no one else was on the road so I would not have an accident. It may seem that God doesn't exist sometimes, but my spirit will not allow me to deny the awesome power of God.

Is it a crime for a man to have nice things? Many of you will say no, if the situation doesn't involve a man of the cloth. But it is a different story when a pastor has the fame, glory and riches. My friend Dean asked me, "How can a pastor drive a nice car, and we have to pay tithes and struggle to make ends meet?" He asked me that question because he and his wife saw a well-known pastor—who has a mega church with a large congregation and often speaks on television—driving a nice SUV with twenty-two-inch rims. Another guy I know had concerns about this same pastor but was a lot harsher. This guy had the nerve to say that he hated "that mother f———," referring to this pastor. I couldn't believe that he would say something like that when he didn't even know the man. Lacking knowledge of God can substantially crack a concrete foundation, and Satan loves when people focus on vanity. God said if we do his will, we shall prosper in every aspect of our lives. Some people look at what others have and become jealous and ungrateful for the things which God has blessed them with. I wonder about people who have a problem with pastors who are blessed. If they were rich, would they consider the poor? If any pastor is willing and strives to achieve his goals, you can't worry about him. God will deal with those who abuse their blessings. God wants to bless you as well, but he can't because your focus is on the wrong thing. God has given all people a measure of faith and knowledge to better themselves, but it is up to each person to do the work needed to succeed. Still, it seems as though when you begin doing something to better yourself, people hate you.

One day during a break at work, I was sitting in my car and writing in my book. One of the supervisors saw me jotting down some notes on my pad. After the break was over, he asked, "What were you writing?" I told him, simply, "Something important." I guess that answer wasn't good enough, or he didn't understand that I didn't want him to know. About five minutes later, he came back, asking me again what I was writing. He even asked if I were writing rhymes for a rap song. That made me feel like he thought it was impossible for a black man to have a desire to write a book. He was very persistent; he even followed me as I walked to my forklift. I refused to tell him what I was writing. Then he said, "You don't want to jinx it by telling me." My response was, "I am not worried about that." But I made a mistake and left my notebook on my forklift the next break. When I remembered, I went out to retrieve it, because I wasn't sure what this person would have done if he'd gotten his hands on it. He'd bugged me so much, but I was unsure why it was so important for him to know what I was doing.

The devil always wants us to do less of what God wants, so that we can do more of what he wants. While I was lying in bed one night, I dreamed about getting up to turn off my bedroom light. When I hit the switch, it wouldn't turn off. I was very frightened because it felt so real. I believe I had that dream because I wasn't studying and reading my Bible as I should have been. My interests were somewhere other than where God wanted them to be, and that was how I realized the meaning of this dream. God got my attention really quickly. After I awoke, I jumped out of bed and started reading a scripture which I had come across several times before but I didn't quite understand. That night God opened my eyes to the meaning of this passage: "And he said, what have you done? The voice of your brother's blood cries out to me from the ground" (Genesis 4:10 NKJV). It refers to Cain killing his brother Abel. God knew what Cain had done; he wanted to see if Cain would tell the truth. Cain killed his brother because he was jealous of him; Abel gave God his best. Cain had that same opportunity to work hard and give God his best. Obedience is the key to changing things, but we must seek God's righteousness. If Cain had done what God asked him to do, his life would have taken a different turn. Read the story for yourself to get a better understanding. And if you do learn from it, take all things into consideration when making choices in your life. I had to make a wise decision at a young age, because I thought if I told anyone what happened, bad things would happen to my family.

When I was about twelve, I was waiting for my oldest sister to finish washing clothes at the Laundromat. While the clothes were drying, my sister used the pay phone across the street. I was watching from the other side. This guy, who everyone knew because it was a small town, wanted to use the phone as well. I could tell he was getting impatient. He got so mad, he called my sister a b———. I was hurt when he called my sister such a degrading name. I wanted to tell my brothers but thought it would cause an uproar between the two families. Everyone in town thought this family was bad and that my family did not take crap either. I couldn't get up the nerve to tell anyone; I didn't even mention it to my sister, because I felt that she would tell my brothers. And they could have hurt someone or gotten hurt if they confronted this guy. And he had a big family, bigger than ours. I just didn't want anything tragic to happen. When I was older, I realized it wasn't my place to say anything, so it took me twenty-five years to tell my sister. You may have seen or heard things that you feel you can't tell anyone. But there will be a time and place when you can tell your story without feeling like the walls are closing in all around you.

Let me reassure you: God is in control of your life, whether you like it or not. The path I wanted to travel had several detour signs, which made me take a different route. I know that you can make stumbling blocks your steppingstones, but these were not those types of blocks. Anytime I wanted to go on that road, my route was cut off. Strange things took place, making it obvious for me to see that wasn't the way to travel. When I was twenty, I would sing at work because I enjoyed singing almost every day. My ex-wife's cousin, Nancy, told me I had a nice voice. One day she asked me for a tape of myself singing; she planned on sending it to BET, which was looking for new talent for a new show. I had a phobia of standing in front of a crowd, but I wasn't going to let that stop me. I took the tape to Nancy but didn't think anything would come of it. I enjoyed the compliments people gave me when they heard me sing.

A few days had passed and the most surprising thing happened: Nancy said they called. I was blown away. The problem was, I was staying with my ex-wife's parents at the time, and they did not have a phone, so Nancy had to leave her number. Nancy said the first time they called her daughter was home alone and had no idea what to say. The second time they called, her husband was at home, and he thought it was a joke. I found it odd that Nancy was never at home to talk to these people so she could relay a message to me.

When I was in the army, some friends and I had started a singing group called Genuine. We practiced for about two weeks. One evening while we were practicing, one of our friends asked if we'd heard this new artist whose name was Genuine. Once we heard that we didn't feel like choosing a new name. We felt that name was a part of us and when it left, so did we.

I used to visit and collaborate with my friend Von. Other people told us we sounded good together. Oftentimes I told Von, "Let's take some time and go to the studio," but every time we tried, something else got in the way. When I was in the army, a guy in my unit said his brother worked with some famous R&B singers; he offered to give my tape to his brother so he could pass it on. The response the guy gave me was that a famous person liked my voice, but he did not give me any contact information. How crazy was that? That was the first time when I felt that God was painting a different picture for my life. God is in control of our lives; it doesn't matter whether or not you know him. He is the head that makes the body move. Don't get me wrong; if you have a desire to dream, by all means, keep pushing.

There was this time when my folks and I were hanging out at a sports bar where a live band was playing. They took a break and asked if anyone wanted to get up and sing. I wanted to see how the crowd would react to me, so I got up the nerve to sing in front of the crowd. They clapped for me, and it felt really good. After it was over, one of the band members asked if I wanted to be in the band. I told him no. I enjoyed singing, but my desire to pursue it professionally was no longer there. I had faced the truth, that dream of me becoming a singer was not happening.

Family members can be your worst and best critics when you are doing something out of the ordinary or that you feel is impossible. But by believing that God is there to carry you through will give you the strength to believe in yourself. One day I went over to my brother Tony's house to visit. I mentioned to him and his wife that I felt happiness and joy when I walked into their house. Tony knew I was writing this book, and he asked when I would let him read it. He and I were in the kitchen; he was cooking, and we were listening to music. I asked Tony to read my book; he said he was about to eat, and he didn't want to at that time. I told him reading one page wouldn't take that much time. He read one page, and then flipped over to the next page. I was very happy when he kept reading; that told me that he enjoyed what I'd written, even though he didn't say one word. I knew that God wanted to take me to higher heights.

I also let his wife, Nina, read a portion of the book, to receive her criticism; every little bit helps. We all went downstairs to watch television, and when I was about to leave, I realized I'd forgotten my book upstairs. As I walked upstairs to retrieve it, I was thinking about telling my sister-in-law to keep me in her prayers so that I'd finish my book. But as I walked through the door, I kept that thought to myself. I no longer felt that I had to say anything to her. And I was amazed when she said, "Joe, keep writing your book." That convinced me to hold on to God and trust him in everything I do. It felt good to talk to Nina about positive things and the power of God. I didn't want to leave! In our next conversation, she told me how hard it was for her after her brother died, and how stressed out she was because of her business. Suddenly, I thought about a scripture, something that would ease her mind. The Word is a great medicine if it is applied properly. When I picked up her Bible, it opened to the scripture I was thinking about; I told Nina it was for her. God uses people to give others hope and inspiration. Hopefully they will take that knowledge and strive harder to believe that he will do what he says he will. Once you live for God, he will always keep you on the right track, even if you don't feel that's where you are. But staying on the right track can be difficult and confusing at times.

Take this example from my church: the men's anniversary was sneaking up on us fast. I had to sing a verse in one of the songs we'd chosen. I practiced my verse over and over again; there was no way I could screw it up. But when it was time to sing, I forgot some of the words. That night I went home, feeling frustrated and like I had nothing to live for, because

I'd wanted to give God my best. The next day I didn't want to think about anything that had happened the night before. I had decided not to attend Bible study school; I was very disappointed with myself. Instead, I waited for the 10:45 a.m. service to begin. Around 10:30 a.m., according to my watch, I left the house to make sure I was on time for the next service. When I had arrived at the church, the Sunday school teacher was still holding class. I looked at my watch, wondering what was going on, because 10:45 a.m. had already passed. One of the deacons came and sat beside me. I asked him, "Are we going to have the next service, and what time will it start?" He gave me a very strange look and said, "You must not have set your clocks back." I was puzzled and thrilled at the same time. I wanted to turn around but it was too late. Bible study was just beginning; it was obvious that God wanted me there even though I'd tried to avoid it.

We must get to know God better; if we do that, it will be easier to recognize when Satan sets a trap. For instance, I was fasting and told myself that I wouldn't eat anything that day. But when I had arrived at work, I remembered that the company ordered pizza whenever we worked overtime on Saturdays. I even told myself that if there were pizza, I still would not eat. During break time, they didn't order pizza. I was happy because there wasn't any pressure. I decided to sit in the break room at a table all alone; I wanted to make sure that I wouldn't be tempted. But I was out of luck. Out of the blue, two guys I knew came over with their food and sat down. That was unusual. I didn't have much to say to the few people who were there, and yet those guys came and sat with me. I didn't even expect for them to come into the break room. I believe Satan was trying to tempt me so I could break my fast, but God kept me strong. One of the guys even offered me some of his food. Whatever you do for God, stay strong and put your trust in him. No matter how bad it may seem, never stop trusting him; I know it does get rough sometimes.

Everything we do affects us in some way. But when God has an effect on you, your whole life begins to change. People look at you differently; depression doesn't take over; and your mind becomes clear, helping you make better choices. You may have thought people were your friends; their cloaks will be uncovered, and they will become your enemies. Let God be effective in your life. When God invests in us, he makes sure his investment is well protected, and he keeps those things and people who may want to harm us in their respective places. And I would like to share a story that relates to this. A female security guard used to work at one of my previous jobs. The first day I saw her I had a positive conversation with her and another security guard, a man. I could tell that the lady security guard took her position too seriously. One day I walked through the scanner with my hands in my pockets, and she told me to go through it again. I had no idea why; maybe she thought I was hiding something. I asked her, "Why do I need to walk through it again?" But without waiting for her response, I went through the scanner again, but angry this time. A few days later, I was called into the office because of that incident. I was angry because I did not do anything wrong. After that, I had several different issues with this guard. When the devil can't get to you one way, he will switch the game on you and try to trap you another way. I started to hate this woman. But I had to come to my senses. I couldn't be a servant for God if I had hate in my heart. So I kept my distance; many times, I didn't even speak to her because she made me just that mad. I know God gave us more strength than that, so I prayed and asked God to stop me from being selfish and not speaking. Eventually, thanks to God, I began to speak to her once again without anger. I knew God would deal with what she'd done to me. And he did! I began to hear rumors that she wouldn't be around much longer. I guess she caused problems with others as well. I am not exactly sure why she was fired, but I was glad she wasn't there to harass me anymore.

The Bible says God will make your enemies your footstool, meaning that when we put on the whole armor of God and trust in him, he gives us the ability to step on the enemy's head. Walking in the power of God helps us to be even closer to him. There may be trouble in some places, but keep stepping. It will give you the opportunity to climb higher.

# CHAPTER 5

# Major Oak

I wonder how I want to be treated, and in return I know how I need to treat others. In my heart, I feel that when issues arise between two people, they should know how to work them out, especially if they are friends. If you have feelings for a person but you have to separate yourself from them for whatever reason, make it a peaceful separation. I am aware that this might be impossible to do in some cases; but if you can, try leaving on good terms.

I allowed Jean to move in with me; he was an associate I'd known for quite some time. When Jean moved in, he began to advise me on some things about the way I was living, because, at that time, I was in bad shape and that affected other parts of my life. I was working but struggling to make ends meet. Jean could see that I was trying to climb out of the hole I'd dug. And when he came to me about something he felt was wrong, I would try to correct it just to avoid confusion and maintain order. When Jean first moved in, my life was in disarray, and his advice was helpful because of what he had been through. We both love God so that we might learn how to love each other—that is my most valuable point.

Jean told me several times that he would do several things for me, not that I was looking for his help. Be careful about how you put words out there, because once they are out, you can't take them back. Jean told me that he would get my motorcycle out of the shop. He also said he would get a lawyer to help me deal with an ordeal. Neither thing ever happened. I didn't really expect him to do those things for me. I was unhappy, however, when I allowed him to use my kitchen for his cooking business, and he didn't pay me anything. But I didn't say anything, because he was trying to better himself and I didn't mind helping him. Thinking about and helping others will take you a long way in life. I don't want to make Jean sound like he was a notorious, coldhearted guy, but somewhere along the line we all get a case of amnesia, forgetting that our purpose is to help others. Jean has done some things for which I was very grateful. But you never know when Satan's words enter into the heart of a man and redirect his thoughts and decisions. The thing that upset me the most was when Jean didn't keep his word. I know that people don't keep their word in everything they say; but breaking your word can be detrimental to the next person and can be a false gesture of love. Jean told me that he would give a month's notice before he vacated the premises; that way, the rent would be covered for the following month. I didn't believe him because of the previous lies; he may have meant well, but he couldn't follow through. A thought of him leaving earlier entered into my mind, and it also became a reality. One day I looked into the refrigerator and noticed all his food was gone. I knew that it wouldn't be long before he followed suit. On the fifth day of the month, I asked if he planned to pay his portion of the rent, and he said yes. After about an hour, Jean came back and told me a man had given him a deal on an apartment that he couldn't refuse. And he would be leaving the next day. I wasn't too pleased because I really needed his help; he was stepping on me when I was already down, and he didn't stick to his word. We must learn to be careful about putting out those words that others can catch. If Jean had told me from the beginning that he was leaving earlier, it wouldn't have been so bad.

Maybe I am just reaping what I have sown in the past. Twice in the Army I roomed with someone else, and I didn't keep my word. The first time, I stayed with this young lady who was moving back to her hometown. She told me to send the rent money to her old address. But I said to myself, *I will never see her again.* The same situation arose when I roomed with Bret. And again, I did not send the money. But there is one thing that occurs to me about Bret. Not only was he a cool white guy, he told me that I could visit him in Florida anytime I wanted to, and I could bring my girlfriend. If I'd only kept my word I could be taking a trip to Florida and would not have to worry about paying for a motel. I wish I'd have sent the young lady her money as well, just because it was the right thing to do.

Not long afterward, Jean told me he would write a check for his portion of the rent. I told him I wouldn't be able to cash the check in time to pay the rent. We'd had this conversation before, but I guess he didn't really care. That night I held my peace, hoping he would change his mind and give me the cash as he'd said he would. The truth of the matter was that he'd never planned to give me cash; he wanted the check to bounce. Without knowing whether God had already prepared someone else to move in with me, he was leaving. The next day, when I came in from work, I noticed some water bottles and three bags of trash sitting outside my apartment door. Inside, I found a note from Jean, telling me to check the mailbox and that he would give me a check when he returned. I was furious because he knew that I couldn't take a check. About 7:00 or 8:00 p.m., Jean walked in the door with a nasty attitude. When I spoke to him in a quiet tone of voice, he responded, "What's up?" He began to move his possessions from the house to his car. He walked back and forth from his car to the house about three times before he asked if I would help him. But the way he asked was very rude so I didn't care to help. Then he had the nerve to say, "If you help, things will move much faster," as if I were the one hurrying him to leave.

Suddenly, I felt sorry for Jean as I watched him take his things up and down the stairs, and I asked if he needed help. But he said no, the first time. Then he changed his mind. I was about to pick something up, and he said, "That's all right." I asked, "What do you want me to do?" He could not make up his mind whether he wanted me to help him or not. He kept walking back and forth to his car. Finally, he went in the house and placed a check on my arm. He said he had to give me a check because he only had about $90 in the bank. I reminded him again that I couldn't take a check. Jean then told me that he would give me cash if I followed him to the bank. I agreed.

When I stepped outside, those bags of trash were still sitting at my door, but he had removed the bottles. I asked Jean, as nicely as I could, if he wanted me to move the trash bags for him. He told me to get away from him. I wondered what was wrong, because I hadn't done anything to provoke him. I even asked him, "What did I do except treat you like a friend?" Jean remained silent until I explained to him again why I couldn't accept a check. Whatever anger that was controlling Jean caused him to walk up to me and push me in my chest. I told him I'd show him I wasn't the person he thought I was, that is, a punk. I told Jean to put up his fists, and we began swinging at each other. Jean almost hit me in my face and when he missed, I swung even harder. Jean got very tired and started to retreat. He was bigger than I was and tired more easily. Once he began to peddle backward, I had the upper hand, and I knew what could happen with the advantage I had gained. Some men would have gotten the best of him. I had to show Jean that I was a man too! I had to step up when adversity arrived.

The good thing about this brawl was that neither one of us touched the other. If I lost control of myself during a fight and did not know when to stop, who knows what may have happened. God wanted me to see that everyone is not your friend. Jean was the type of person who thought he could push me around; he thought he was superior and stronger because he was bigger. But he was not smarter. God not only showed him some things about me, he showed me some things about Jean. The best passage for me to describe this event is Psalm 55:12–14:

> For it is not an enemy who reproaches me; then I could bear it. Nor is it one who hates me who has exalted himself against me; But it was you, a man my equal, my companion and acquaintance. We took sweet counsel together, and walked to the house of God in the throng. (NKJV)

In this passage, David states that he sat down with someone who he knew had stabbed him in the back. He even went to church with this person and they tried to saves souls together. Anyone that is close to you can seem like the enemy.

There is one last thing I want to say about Jean. Many years passed, and I had pretty much forgotten about him. But one day I was taking a break at a truck stop and someone grabbed me by the arm. I had no idea who it might be. When I looked over my left shoulder, there was Jean, smiling in my face. He even hugged me, like he was glad to see me. But I wasn't too thrilled to see him, because I didn't want to be friends with a person who didn't know how to treat me. He gave me his phone number, but it didn't do any good; I'd made up my mind! Be careful about how you treat your friends because you may lose them for good.

"Behold, I send you forth as sheep in the midst of wolves: be ye therefore wise as serpents, and harmless as doves" (Matthew 10:16 KJV). One day I passed through an unfamiliar neighborhood. There was a basketball court near a church, and I'd promised myself that I would play there one day. That day arrived; the sun was out and I had nothing else to do, so I decided to check out this court. I had no problem going to other places to play basketball because I loved the sport that much. When I arrived, there were a few people on the court playing, which made it even better. In the first game, my teammates and I dominated the other team. But before we could finish that game, a dark-skinned guy walked up and said that he had down next. Once the next game began, the guy who had down was guarding me. I wasn't too pleased at the way he guarded me because he pushed me while I was standing under the goal. Basketball is a physical game, but I really didn't want to get too sweaty. When I said something to the guy, he got mad at me, and we exchanged words. We argued back and forth; then he said if I said one more word, he would slap me in my mouth.

At that moment, all kinds of things ran through my mind. First, what would happen to my friend's jeep if the guy and I fought, and I kicked his butt. Perhaps one day my friend would be riding in his jeep and the guy would see him; who's to say what might take place, or what if one of the guy's friends jumped me from behind. After this guy shamed me in front of all those people, I felt bad about myself. I'd wanted to fight, but instead of playing into the hands of the enemy, I refused and walked away. I still felt like a punk, even though I knew that it is the bigger man who walks away from a fight.

I was so confused I talked to my brother Tony, hoping he could ease the hurt. Tony said I'd done the right thing by walking away. He made me feel somewhat better. If you are provoked to engage in a fight, walk away if you can; it doesn't mean you are a punk. By all means, if you have to, defend yourself; if fighting is the only way, then handle your business. God gave me the wisdom and strength to make the right decision that day; it made me less than a man for a while, but I got over it. I was humble and wise in the midst of the wolves.

One day, my coworker Drieck asked his line leader if he could drive the forklift to help pull some orders. He was told that the company wouldn't train him to drive a lift, because he didn't need to do so for his job. But Drieck wanted the experience; if things had changed in his life, he would have something else to fall back on. Fortunately, the day came when he had the chance to drive a lift. I was pulling orders that included a lot of televisions. He asked a line leader if he could help me move the televisions from the racks to the staging point. When Drieck pulled the televisions from the lower rack onto the floor, he had no problems. But when he had to go up to one of the higher racks, he quit and went back to his main job. I asked him what was wrong, and he said he was afraid of dropping a television. And he was right; there was a great chance of that. The truth of the matter is that trial and error is the key. Drieck should have given his best and not worried about dropping a television. The company had insurance. His chance of success was greater because I was there to help him. But when things become too hard, we give up too easily.

You will get butterflies before you embark on any new thing, and that is natural. But after you have done it for a while, and through trial and error, it will become easier. It takes time to learn anything, from riding a bike to driving a car, but once you learn it, no one can take it from you. Many times the reason why we can't accomplish more in life is because we have carnal minds instead of spiritual minds. A carnal mind causes you to think like a natural man, who has no ambitions of his own. But the man who is spiritually-minded can counsel himself while striving toward his goals. And don't forget that God said that we can do all things through Christ Jesus who strengthens us.

One night, I was heading home from work. I was traveling on a particular road, trying to avoid roadblocks because my license had been suspended. But on this night, the thing from which I was trying to escape was like a ghost that hunted me down. As I came up to a red light, I saw blue lights flashing on and off like a Christmas tree. Every time I see those lights, I get paranoid. Turning left would have put me very close to my place of residence, but nothing I did would have kept the officer from getting suspicious. In the past, I would have turned into someone else's driveway. But the first time I tried that, it didn't work; the police went to where I was and still wrote me up. I didn't want to get caught doing that same thing, I had to trust God and hope that he'd provided a way for me to escape. And sure enough he did; while I was making the left turn, I noticed that at every other point there was an officer stopping cars. But no one was checking the point to my left. To whom else can you give the credit but God? Yes, it may seem like there is trouble in front of us, but God has made a way for his people. Even when we fail to obey God's commandments, he still is in the blessing business.

A sign from God is not an illusion; it can be motivation to change bad habits. I used to drink with my nephew from time to time. I didn't want to get hooked on it, but then I began dating a young lady who drank as well, which made it easier for me to indulge. I began drinking almost every day, as long as it was in my presence. I thought I needed it, because it kept my mind off things I didn't want to think about. As time went on, I asked myself if I'd ever have the power to reject this habit? God purposely kept the idea of rejection on my mind. I can't speak for anyone else, and I don't know how many people are honest about their problems. But for me, it was and still is a struggle to just give it up for good. At times, I feel as though I am glued to my decision to quit but sometimes that glue has no ability to hold anything together. God loves us so much that he gives us clear signs to help us avoid or control temptation. In my case, the sign was my nephew telling me he'd stopped drinking. I was stunned because my nephew drank like liquor was fuel for living. He had gotten his commercial driver's license and didn't want to risk losing them by getting a DUI. His quitting made me reconsider my future: if I didn't take control over this habit, God wouldn't give me what my heart desired. I believe God used my nephew to help me deal with my habit.

> I went by the field of the slothful, and by the vineyard of the man void of understanding; And, lo, it was all grown over with thorns, and nettles had covered the face thereof, and the stone wall thereof was broken down. Then I saw, and considered it well: I looked upon it, and received instruction. (Proverbs 24:30–32 KJV)

Think about what others are dealing with, and you may learn many things about your own life, which in fact may help you.

My friend Edmond told me about a Christian lady who owned her own business. However, most people shopped at the store next to hers. The woman fasted and prayed that God would fix this problem, but nothing changed. I was eager to know why she wasn't attracting customers to her store. Edmond said she had a nasty attitude with her customers. A good attitude can cause great things to happen in your life, and a bad one can cause havoc and keep your heart from accepting constructive criticism. A bad attitude can keep someone from loving you and your children from respecting you or others, because they do what their parents do. You will be impatient and likely will hang around with those who hide themselves in sheep's clothing. Such an attitude can turn a beautiful swan into an ugly duckling, but most important, it will make you reject God and his ways.

Learn how to be thankful! One evening a coworker named Sandy was complaining because the supervisor had asked everyone to work on a Saturday. I asked her, nicely, what if they told us they were laying everybody off? It made her see things differently, and she didn't have much to say after that. I knew how it felt to be out of work. At one point, I was out of work for almost a year, and it nearly drove me crazy. I didn't go into detail with her, but she agreed it would be bad. Sandy then talked about visiting her hometown. As I rode away from her on the forklift, a thought entered my mind: she had a son. I had no idea whether or not she had one, but God did. I rode back over to Sandy and asked if she were visiting her son in her hometown, and she said yes. After I left Sandy the second time, she came over to me and asked, "How did you know I had a son?" I said God told me to tell her that her son would be all right. Sandy then wanted to tell me something that had happened in the past. I didn't have time to listen then, but I asked her to write it down, and I would share her story of how God was present in her life with the world. I left her with these words: "When you have more love for something or someone else than God, there is neither resting place nor peace."

A few days had passed before Sandy gave me what she wrote. The first story was about an abusive relationship. She wanted to leave but knew she wouldn't be able to do it on her own, so she prayed and asked God to help her. All day she prayed to God to help her do the right thing—either leave or go. That evening when her boyfriend came home, she packed her clothes and put her bags in the car. She left and headed toward her son's house but pulled the car over more than five times, intending to go back to her boyfriend. But every time, her focus remained on her son. Sandy knew that God was guiding her just like she had asked him to.

Sandy's next story occurred on July 23, 1984. Her son Joseph died at the age of eight. At that time, she also had a twelve-year-old and a ten-year-old. Her ten-year-old son had been with Joseph when a horrific accident happened. The ignorant adults in the neighborhood later asked her son why he let his baby brother die, making him believe it was his fault that his brother died. One day, he asked if he could visit some friends for the weekend, elderly folks who were close to the family. She didn't see anything wrong with that, and let him go. Around 3:00 a.m. her phone rang; it was her son on the other end. He was hysterical, and it took her about ten minutes to calm him down and find out what was wrong. He said something had awakened him. He sat up in the bed. In the doorway there was a bright light staring him in the face, and he saw Joseph. He sat on the edge of the bed, and Joseph walked over to him and sat on his lap, hugging him and saying he loved him. And in a twinkling of an eye, he was gone. Sandy told her son that God knew he blamed himself for his brother's death, but it wasn't his fault. After her son had this dream, he never worried about what people said. I think it helped him get over the insults from neighbors.

I can't stand when undeveloped Christians want to control other people's property. Let me explain. I called a Christian TV channel and spoke to a woman on the phone. I called to ask someone to pray for me, because I was facing adversities that had messed me up. After some time, this woman and I began talking on a regular basis, but she didn't want to meet face-to-face immediately. We did meet about five months later. We were in the car one day, and I turned to an R&B music station. She demanded that I turn it off. Since I am a gentleman, I turned it to a gospel station to make her feel better. I didn't think it was wrong to listen to R&B music. Many guys would have turned the car around and told her to get out. The thing that got me was why someone would demand that I do something with my stuff. There is a way of asking a person to do something, and they may not have a problem doing what you ask, but, being demanding toward someone else's property, that might get you cursed out, for real. I believe she was being selfish in this situation, and being selfish will get you nowhere fast. Be advised, Christians, everything we deal with will not be to our satisfaction. Many times we just have to let things remain as they are, because they are not our battles to fight. Otherwise, you may have to think twice about dealing with another person. As Christians, we do have boundaries that we must not cross, even though some people cross them anyways. Here is a tip: there is nothing to gain by crossing boundaries, and if you do gain anything, you will only have it for a little while.

I was willing to be a friend to this woman, but after she turned out to be so demanding, I didn't care if the relationship ended at that very moment. Still, I tried to maintain some type of friendship with her, then had second thoughts when she showed up at my house without calling. I had to draw the line because I wasn't sure what she was trying to do, but it was a turnoff.

For whatever reason, it seems as though it is hard for one man to tell another man that he loves him, and that doesn't mean they are gay. I had to speak one Saturday at the men's breakfast and was thinking about what God wanted me to speak on. I had two weeks to prepare my speech. I looked over some scriptures that I had already written down in my notes. I wasn't comfortable speaking about them nor was I sure if I understood them enough. The next day at work, I passed one of my coworkers in the forklift and did not stop to hold a conversation with him. I quickly said, "Man, I love you." About ten minutes later, I walked up to another coworker and shook his hand. He pulled me closer and, embracing me, said, "Man, give me some love." God didn't have to say or show me anything else because I knew that was what he wanted me to speak about—men having love for men. Loving your father is no different from loving another man, whom you should see as a brother. If men can't show love and respect to each other, then how can they show love to a woman? Having sex with a woman is not the same as loving her. Jesus was a man who died for mankind and that is a love no one can truly understand. God wants men to come together and learn from one another, because that will make us all a better man. In the Bible, God speaks about love: how can you love me, whom you've never seen, and hate your brother, whom you see every day? When I was younger, there were two brothers; one was short and the other was very tall. They got into an altercation because the taller brother owed the shorter brother a dollar. And the shorter one shot and killed his brother over one dollar. I want to be sociable and say that we have more sense than that, but how can I when the truth is staring me in the face. Learn to love your brothers. It is difficult, because there is too much hating going on. But stop worrying about what another man has and what you don't have. Ask God to take away the malicious heart that causes people to withdraw from you and replace it with a heart that knows how to love.

One day, right before an 8:00 a.m. meeting, Edmond said, "If the forklift happens to roll through the dock doors, don't jump off." I wasn't sure why he said that; evidently he knew something I didn't. About thirty minutes later, Edmond drove into a straight truck; it moved forward, and he went out the door on the forklift. Two weeks later, the incident was still on my mind. I couldn't grasp what had happened. One day Edmond and I were working together, and I had to ask him, "Why did that happen to you?" He told me that God would give me the answer soon enough.

The topic came up again on another day, and this time Edmond went into more detail. He had asked the driver if it were safe to go into his truck, and the driver told him yes. He even asked the group leader, just to make sure. But as Edmond was unloading the last pallet from the truck, the driver removed the chock block from the wheel, which caused the truck to roll away. Some of the head people came to find out what had happened and why. The plant manager was very upset with Edmond and asked, "Who told you to drive the forklift into the smaller truck?" Edmond said his group leader had said it was okay. When the manager questioned the group leader, he said, "You can drive a lift into a smaller truck if its wheels are chocked."

My point is that we go through things that may not be meant for us. However, we may be used to prevent others from getting hurt. Edmond did the right thing by staying on the lift and not jumping off. A coworker and I said we would have jumped off the lift, and we could have been crushed to death. God had to ensure it was done the right way to show others what to do in that situation. We needed to trust what our eyes had seen and know that we can learn by example.

Doesn't it anger you when people think they know more about your life than you do? I know the answer to that question is yes! Something very discomforting took place while I was dating a young lady named Shelia. One night as I was urinating I felt a burning sensation that would not go away. My first thought was to fly into a rage and ask Shelia if she'd been messing around, but I knew that wouldn't get me anywhere. However, I felt that there was a great chance that she had been cheating. I knew for a fact that I wasn't the one who was going outside the relationship. Instead of getting angry, I told Shelia we both needed to go to the hospital.

When we arrived, they put us in two separate rooms. I was both calm and angry because, as I said before, I hadn't done anything. But I didn't get irate until this black doctor walked into the room and asked me, "Man, what have you done?" That really got my blood boiling to the point where I wanted to say something that wasn't nice. I had thought a professional doctor would know to keep his nose out of other people's business, but I was wrong. I hadn't given him one reason to suspect that I had messed around on Shelia. This doctor was on the outside looking in, wondering who the culprit was. I was madder at him than I was at my current situation. I knew it would be taken care of with a shot of penicillin, but in my case it was a long Q-tip inserted into my penis, and it hurt like hell. I guess he had many cases in which the men were guilty. But the question he asked made me feel worse than if I'd been hit by a Mack truck. It would be a different story if people could place themselves in the shoes of others. They would retrieve their thoughts and words before they speak. Sometimes I think they don't know when they say degrading things, because Satan makes them think that they are right every time they open their mouths. That is why we must strive to do our best and get to know God better, so we will have the knowledge to counteract Satan's desire to make us hurt one another. God wants laborers who can hear his voice when he speaks and determine when Satan tempts them to be sidewinders. "Then he said to them, the harvest truly is great, but the laborers are few; therefore pray the Lord of the harvest to send out laborers into his harvest" (Luke 10:2 NKJV). God loves when his people know what he wants them to do and are obedient.

Let me explain one thing about being obedient: if your heart and conscience convince you to do something that might not feel right, and you take heed, that is a form of obedience. One Friday evening before I got off from work, I asked Tom, the plant manager, if some of us could work at a different plant on Saturday. I wanted to work extra hours and use the money to pay some bills. Keep in mind that I had already put in a lot of hours that week; I was determined to make even more. Only a few guys wanted to work; it was voluntary. Before the end of the workday, Tom asked Randy if he had a key to the office so that I and the other guys could clock in and get our truck keys for Saturday. Randy had been there the longest; maybe that was the reason he was asked if he had a key. Of course, I wondered why Tom didn't ask me, because I closed the plant most of the time. But that is another story, and it doesn't pertain to the issue of being obedient. I stood there and watched the keys exchanged from one hand to the next, wondering why I didn't get them. But I was more concerned about the fact that I would be getting more hours and more money. And as soon as I left work, I went straight to church for choir practice, even though I had worked fourteen hours that day and was very tired. When I finally made it home, I didn't have time to do anything but take a shower and go to bed.

As Saturday morning came closer and closer, I wanted so much to change my mind. I was just that tired. But I couldn't, because I had given my word that I would be at work. I felt that God wanted me to put in those extra hours to pay more of my bills. I jumped up out of my bed before the alarm clock could sound and went to work. I was the first one there, as I was every other day. I was even there before the guy with the keys to the office, but he showed up about ten minutes later. Randy got out of his car and started his truck, without opening the office to get his truck keys. I proceeded to walk alongside him to get into the office to warm up and get my keys. Randy asked me if I knew the code to the office alarm, and I said no. I got back into my car so I could stay warm. He walked over to my car and said that the plant manager could write our time in on Monday, but that wasn't the main issue for me. Randy didn't know that my truck key was inside the office, which was where everyone was supposed to leave his keys at the end of the day. I sat there for a while, wondering if anyone else would show up with the code to the security alarm. By this time, there were three of us there; one guy was new, and he didn't know the code. What made me obey God, was when I noticed the new guy started his truck without going into the office. I was the only one who hadn't taken his keys with him on Friday evening. It made no sense for me to keep waiting around, and anyway I was exhausted. I truly believe that God wanted me to go home and get some rest and not worry about making more money just to pay some bills. You can have all the money in the world, but it can't take you to that place of refuge.

This is an example of a person who works quietly but can be very treacherous if he wants to harm you. My employers wanted us to volunteer to work on a Thanksgiving Day. I didn't mind because I had no plans to do anything. When I arrived at work that morning, I was about two minutes late, for which employees usually earned a demerit. I asked the supervisor if I would receive a demerit for being a bit late. And he said no, because I had volunteered to work on a holiday. But that attitude changed when things weren't going in his favor. Some of my coworkers had made it clear that they would leave at noon, and he was okay with that. When 2:00 p.m. came around, others began to leave without warning the supervisor. Then it became a problem, because there was work that needed to be finished. Never did I think to leave or tell him I wanted to leave at a certain time; I was there for the duration. But the supervisor walked over to me and said, "Joe, you know if you leave, I will have to give you a demerit." I told him I didn't want to leave anyway. He responded, "I thought you were one of the ones who wanted to leave early." "Behold, I send you out as sheep in the midst of wolves. Therefore be wise as serpents and harmless as doves" (Matthew 10:16 NKJV). God sometimes sends us out in the midst of the wolves just so we can see how his spirit controls our every move. The supervisor made it seem like I wanted to leave, but he only wanted to scare me into staying. How crazy does that sound? It makes no sense to me.

Why be afraid to be in the shadow of your sister or brother who is in the limelight? Let me explain. A friend named Ann asked me out to dinner one night. When I arrived, Ann's roommate was also sitting at the table. She seemed rather distant. Later Ann told me her roommate acted that way because she didn't want me to know to whom she was related. I was a little disturbed because it didn't matter to me. Ann's roommate had a sister who was a well-known gospel singer. I thought it was ridiculous to be jealous of one's sister because she was famous. People don't care who you are unless they are trying to use you. Everyone has something going on in his or her life and doesn't have time to worry about what is or isn't going on in someone else's. Life isn't always easy, but the strong will survive. We can't give into fear and stop what God wants to happen. If that lady had focused more on herself and did not allow fear to hinder her, she too would be successful. More than a couple of times, I got up to speak and my words left me. I forgot what I wanted to say because of fear. But I kept getting up, knowing that God would deliver me from this phobia someday. "I sought the Lord, and he heard me, and delivered me from all my fears" (Psalms 34:4 KJV). This passage reminds me of things we should not fear: being broke, losing worldly possessions, being lonely, trusting God with all our hearts, stepping out on faith, loving and being loved, being chastised, being let down, letting go, suffering, surrendering, waiting, not knowing the outcome, going after what your heart desires, living, dying, communicating, moving, standing still, responsibilities, learning, making mistakes, the dark and the light, being filled by the Holy Spirit, fighting, war and peace, speaking one's mind, aging, falling, getting up, the past, the future, giving, receiving, change, the truth, expanding, forgiving, gaining wealth, doubt, believing, persecution, opposition, commitment, dedication, the enemy, slipping, taking control, and most of all, loving God.

# CHAPTER 6

# Royal Oak

You can't hinder your opportunities by waiting on friends who are trying to be successful. In fact, waiting on others will only stop your blessings. I had a friend whose nickname was Miz, and whenever he visited, we always talked about doing big things with our lives. Miz was working hard as a rapper, trying to get a record deal. He'd tell me that if he made it big, he'd hook me up as well, because I was his friend. And the more I heard those words, the lazier I became, letting my dreams of writing go to waste. Then one day God spoke to me and said if I could wait on man, then surely I could work hard and wait for my own dreams to come to pass, because man would always disappoint me. I was standing still, waiting for Miz to make it big, and nothing was happening. I even stopped writing my book, hoping that my blessings would come through Miz. But that didn't keep Miz and me from being friends. It wasn't my intention to leech off him if he did make it, but I won't lie, it would have been nice. I came to my senses and realized that God gave me the ability to dig deep inside myself and know that the blessings I will receive will come because I work hard and trust that he will bring them to pass. Miz telling me what he would do for me when he made it threw a wrench in my plans and almost put a halt to my progress. Do not wait for anyone to give you what your heart desires; go out and get it for yourself. You will cherish it much more than if it is handed to you on a platter.

As it turned out, I moved and never knew what happened to Miz. I don't think he made it in the music business; I haven't seen or heard anything about him. Now, if I'd kept waiting on Miz, I would still be wondering, *What if I'd kept writing my book? Who knows what might have happened?*

Getting to know new people can be a drag sometimes, because you never know what to expect. Once they show their true colors, you might not want to hang with them again. During my time in the army, some new recruits came to my unit one day. They wanted to hang out and ride around town later on that evening. I didn't have my car, so I decided to ride with them, because I didn't want to be a drag and not show them around town. I usually took my car because I hate riding with other people; sometimes they don't want to leave when you do. After we saw all of Fort Bragg, I took them to a motel with a club. We were only there for about an hour or two; maybe they didn't like the club and that was the reason we didn't stay longer. We'd walked into the club one way and left another way. As we were walking out through the lobby of the motel, one of the guys noticed a house made out of clear plastic, about thirty-six by forty-two inches in size. It had some money inside it, donations for some organization, probably no more than twenty-five dollars. I kept walking as if I hadn't seen it, because the money wasn't worth going to jail. But two of the guys said they were going to steal the house. I began to walk faster; I no longer wanted to be associated with these nuts. While the youngest guy and I were waiting for them to come out, I asked why he liked hanging with the other two. I can't remember what his response was, but he seemed like a pretty good kid. Not long afterward, those two fools ran out with the house in their hands, screaming, "Joe, start the car!" I couldn't believe they'd stolen the money and put me and this younger guy in danger. It was obvious they didn't care for anyone else but themselves. From that day forward, I never rode with those guys again, because if anyone had called the police, we all would have gone to jail. And I know that they would have put some of the blame on me.

If you hang out with someone and see them doing things that are wrong, do yourself a favor—leave quickly and never return. Eventually, they will get caught, and if you are with them, there is a great chance you will go down too. They are not going to stop just because you don't do it. If anything, they will encourage you to go along with them. Don't allow people to drag you into something you don't want to be in, and certainly don't be anyone's fool.

This next story is a good example of what happens when you are not careful and trust new people too quickly. The results can be fatal. This story was on the local news and occurred not far from my hometown. A guy at a club had been drinking; I'm not sure whether or not he was drunk. A girl walked up to him and asked if he wanted to go to a house party. He told her yes. Perhaps they talked for a while, and that made him feel more comfortable around her. Once they arrived at the house party, the young man drank all the liquor he wanted. The next morning he woke up in a tub of ice; a phone was in arm's reach and a message was written on the mirror. The message told him to call the police, which freaked him out. After he'd fallen asleep, some college kids took out his kidneys. They planned to sell his kidneys to whoever would buy them. Please, stay alert when you meet new people, no matter what they look like. Beauty can sometimes be a trap, just to lure you in.

Be cautious whenever you think about leaving your kids alone in the car. One day I pulled into the parking lot of a grocery store. I parked alongside a car with two adorable little girls sitting in the back; the car was running. Being warmhearted and having a concern for others, I couldn't leave until their parents returned to the car. I even asked a few people if the car was theirs. After awhile, I saw a young lady walking toward the car. I told her she should be more careful and not leave her kids by themselves in the car. She said she hadn't planned to be in the store that long, they'd been sleep, and it was too much of a hassle to take them inside with her. I told her, "It only takes a few minutes for someone to steal your car and kids." I think the real issue was that she was too lazy to gather her kids and take them into the store. I have heard numerous stories about people who have left their kids in their running cars, and someone has taken both. Before I let her go, I asked the young lady, "Would you rather have someone steal your car or both your car and your kids? You can replace a car if it gets stolen, but you can't replace your kid." I hoped that would make her think twice next time.

Oftentimes we are fooled into thinking people care for us, that is, until they have no more use for us. I have seen it with my own eyes: people throw you to the dogs when you no longer benefit them. My brother Johnny played football in high school, and he was pretty good. The principal gave money to any player who would sack the quarterback. And I am pretty sure my brother got his share, because I can recall how many times his name was called on a play for making a tackle. But about three years or so after my brother was out of school, Johnny and I rode to the game one night and sat in the parking lot with the music blasting. That same principal called the police on my brother, and they took him to jail. I believe the principal could have handled this situation better; he had known my brother for many years. He could have asked my brother to turn down his music. I was young at that time and I didn't quite understand what had happened until God allowed my mind to accept the reality of it. My point is, don't be too gullible and believe that a certain person cares a great deal about you. And I'm not saying my brother was gullible, because he also got something from that principal every time he tackled the quarterback. I am just speaking in general, because there are many people who love to use this approach to get what they want when they want it.

At one point, I wanted to stop paying for a car. I'd fallen behind on the payments because I didn't handle my business properly. There was a time when I was behind at least five payments. I wasn't sure if or when they would repossess it. But I kept my faith in God and knew that one day I would pay it off. It is far beyond my thinking how God allowed me to keep my car. The things we want to happen don't happen overnight, but if we keep God as the head of our lives and patiently wait and be more aggressive about what we want, we just might get it. Only God knows what is best for us; remember that when things don't take place at a particular time. If you believe in God, show him that you will abide in him as he will abide in you. Be strong and of good courage; you will need both to remain under his covering. Aggressiveness can be a great thing, depending on how and when you use it. If you are too aggressive, things can or may not go the way you want them to. Learn how to harness this aggressiveness to prevent it from turning into anger.

When I was younger, my dad bought land from some people who lived on a field across from our residence. And, as far as I can remember, we had a trailer home on part of that land. My dad said that one day he would build a house on a different part. We owned about one acre, and it was a nice piece of land. When we lived in the trailer home, we had no problem with anyone. But then my father built our brick house. And Mr. Wendell, a white man in the neighborhood, concocted a surprise for my whole family. He placed a barbed-wire fence in front of our house where his land started and ours ended. The division of land hadn't been an issue until he put up the fence. We were all in a rage, but only a few wanted to act on that rage. Some of my brothers and I started to tear down the fence, but our dad wouldn't allow it. It was evident that our father was much wiser than we were, because he knew that something worse could have followed our actions.

Not long after the fence went up, Mr. Wendell placed three large and broken-down pieces of equipment in front of our home. I guess he decided the fence didn't make us react in an idiotic way, so he had to try something more sinister. We ignored the fence; if we wanted to cross to the other side, we just simply stepped over it. And the large equipment became our playground. We played tag on these machines as if we were at the playground. We were in the country, so we didn't have many choices about how to entertain ourselves. We did the next best thing—improvise. We still do not know why Mr. Wendell wanted to humiliate us; but he only made us see more vividly rather than be blinded by our own anger. "Do not rejoice when your enemy falls, and do not let your heart be glad when he stumbles" (Proverbs 24:17 NKJV). That is what we do when people do us wrong; once they have fallen, we laugh at them. We gain nothing when we have that eye-for-an-eye syndrome. Even though Mr. Wendell clearly hated us, I never heard my mother or father talk about him when the word was out that his wife was cheating on him with a black man. I had some pretty classy parents. Someone else probably would have retaliated, making themselves no better than the enemy.

It doesn't take much for us to be encouraged about things that are righteous. It becomes hard when we don't hold fast to the words of righteousness. One night I was watching a movie with a sergeant speaking to his soldiers. He told them if they put away their emotions, they would become winners. I feel the same about Christians: if we put away negative emotions, then we can be winners for Christ. Our love for God should be the strongest emotion we allow in our heart and cherish it until we pass from this life; that way we won't rejoice when our enemies fall, because that will have nothing do with God.

Parents have their way of getting your attention, but when the parental way is not effective, God must intervene. And most of the time, his way is much harsher than the parent's way. One of my neighbors, who passed away many years ago, was dealing with several issues. God got his attention by allowing him to go to jail, without being sure if he would get out. When he was in jail, he cried out to God on his knees. Many of you will not have to face what this guy was facing, if only you will take heed. Some of you are already there, but God is there as well, ready to ease your minds and wipe your slates clean. But you must be ready and willing to follow the yellow brick road that will guide you to your destiny.

Once God had to get my attention; it wasn't a good experience, but I understood the reason. I had let an altercation go too far, which landed me into jail. I had not planned to stay in the "Plaza Hotel" long, but my stay was extended without my consent. I didn't think I would be there that long, until I heard from another guy that they were getting ready to issue uniforms. Plus, they removed us from the holding cell. I was frightened and frustrated at the same time, because I thought I was being railroaded. But what could I do except remain calm? I knew that my family would come through and get me out of jail. While we were standing in line, one of the officers asked if anyone wanted a Bible to read. At first I thought I would get one, but I was too upset and went straight to my cell. My situation didn't make me want to read the Bible, even though it was the best thing for me. I should have taken the Bible just in case I wanted to read it, after my frustration had disappeared. God overrode my distress and filled my heart with joy. And God made provisions for me to read his Word, even when I didn't feel like it. When I opened the door to my cell I was astonished to see a Bible lying on the table, open as if it were waiting for me. God is wonderful, but sometimes he shows it in a strange way. My cell mate came in about an hour after I entered the cell; he was a young man around the age of twenty-four. When he walked in, I was reading the Bible, and he told me it belonged to him, but he was cool about me using it. This young man and I had a long conversation about God and life, and talking to him kept my mind off the fact that I was in jail. The first night he wanted to talk the whole night, until I told him I needed to get some sleep.

The next day I read the Bible once again; it seemed as though God was speaking and informing me that was the way he wanted me to read the Bible. It was easy for me to get distracted at home. In jail, it wasn't easy for me to jump up at any time and do what I wanted. God got my attention the best way he knew how to teach me about conviction. How can you be a minister who does not want to study and say your heart is fully devoted to God? On that day, I did the same as I had the first day, hoping my name would be called and I'd be released. But on the third day, while I was reading my Bible, I was glad to hear God's spirit reassuring me in a soft voice that I wouldn't be there much longer. I had high hopes, so I just kept reading the Bible. I tried not to focus on what one of the inmates was saying, that it took two or three months just to get on the list for the work-release program. Praying and reading the Bible, I remained positive, even though I did not know what the outcome would be. But I sure didn't want to be there too much longer. Not long afterward, my name was called, and I was told to gather my things because it was time to leave. After getting out of there, I read my Bible even more. I wanted to show God that I was worthy of his many blessings. One way or another, I would be a servant for him.

Stop allowing Satan to make you think that your burdens are too heavy. Trust me, I know they seem that way most of the time, but turn them over to God; they're nothing to him. Think about picking up something that weighs two hundred pounds. It would be very difficult to lift it, depending on your weight and size. The way you decide to lift this weight can make a great difference in the end result. If your burden becomes too heavy, allow God to be the pulley that makes it easier for you to lift it or let it down. It's not good to keep doing things on your own; without God you will continue to struggle and will not reach your goals. God gave me this metaphor in a dream, and dreams can be very important on this life journey. They come from the Holy Spirit, which guides us when we feel lost or are about to enter into new territory. In my dream, a coworker directed me to a piece of metal that looked too heavy to lift. He told me he could lift it but not by his own strength. My coworker then hooked this piece of metal to a chain and ran the chain through a pulley, which made sense. It gave him the leverage he needed to reach his goal. And in life, God is the leverage needed to carry our heavy load, but there are other things that can sustain you. For instance, my brother Willie was in jail for eighteen months for something I don't want to disclose. Instead, expressing his anger against his cell mates, he lifted weights, which kept his mind off thoughts that could have destroyed his life. If you are going through some rough times, don't just sit there waiting for them to consume you. Get up and do something. Place yourself in a different situation. It will alter your current one; if you deal with the problem, it no longer has priority over your life.

Have you ever thought about the different things going on in the world and said, *Where do I fit in all of this?* I have wondered this many times and concluded that God wants his people to have a better understanding of this world and be removed from its wicked, dark, and deceptive delusions. Many times, it seems as though this world has a lot to offer a man or woman, but that means nothing to God. "He who loves his life will lose it, and he who hates his life in this world will keep it for eternal life" (John 12:25 NKJV). I can name several different ways that a man can lose his life and maybe his soul, if he's not careful about what he does with it. One thing made me cautious about what I did and where and with whom I did it. And that was gambling, because my dad showed me that he despised cards. One night my sister Debra and I were gambling for pennies; my dad must have known that we were doing something that was against his will. He walked into the living room where we were, but before he could see exactly what we were doing, we both hid the cards under our legs. Of course, parents are much smarter than kids. My father told me to get up and put a chair up to the dining table. I told him I would get it later. He insisted that I move the chair right then. I couldn't defy my father. As I got up, the card fell from under my leg, and my dad was frustrated. I was surprised that my sister and I didn't get a beating that night. Who knows? Maybe my father had experienced something bad in the past or witnessed someone being murdered due to gambling. At the time, I couldn't understand why my father was so against his children playing with a deck of cards. As an older man I have seen and heard some things about cards and gambling. My friend Nick says it is hard for him to give up gambling because he has been doing it for so long. To transcend takes a lot of concentration and hard work; need I say more?

We try to tell people things for their own good, but often they do not listen because they don't believe what we are telling them is true. They may even think we dislike them because we have shared our feelings and thoughts in an attempt to help them. When someone is telling me something that will help me, I listen because I don't want to face the same hell they faced. No matter what people tell you, it still may feel like your season is not coming to pass. But God is waiting on you to do what it takes to have an abundant life.

For example, I got my car out of the shop one Saturday morning, and the battery wouldn't stay charged. Later that night I drove it for a while, hoping that would charge the battery, because I really wanted to go to church on Sunday. The next morning, I tried to start my car, and it wouldn't start. I was very disappointed. For a moment, I just stood there, thinking about what I could do and giving up at the same time. A thought entered my mind that if my roommate were coming around the corner, I could get him to take me. And right after I had that thought, I couldn't believe my eyes—my roommate was coming around the corner. I didn't expect God to move that fast. When you feel like you have done everything and you have no other options, God will step in and work it out. The question is, are you willing to hold on to God's hand until he works it out? And after he has you by the hand, don't let go, because you'll be right back where you started.

Searching for true love can be a headache at times. You may have to be imaginative and try new ways to find someone. Sometimes you may not want to pursue anyone, because starting over can be a drag as well. But searching can be even worse, because you don't know what to expect. Always expect the unexpected; it will keep you levelheaded. One morning I was watching television, and I saw a dating-service phone number come across the screen. I had seen it before but never cared to write it down. But that day I decided to try my luck and see where it would lead me. I called that night and talked to a woman whose voice sounded so soft and sweet. At times, this woman and I talked for hours on the phone. The topics we discussed and her attentiveness made our conversations more interesting, because sometimes it's difficult for other people to understand things the way you do. We decided to send each other pictures of ourselves.

After a few days had passed, I had received her picture, but she hadn't received mine. I couldn't see how that was possible because I'd sent my picture first. After a few more days, this woman asked me where my picture was. A few more days later, she called, telling me to confess. I asked, "For what?" She assumed I'd tricked her into sending her picture first, so I could see what she looked like; if she didn't look nice, then I wouldn't send her a picture of myself. But it wasn't anything like that; in fact I didn't understand why she never got my picture. It occurred to me that God wanted me to separate myself from her. I say that because of what she said she would do to me because of this picture. Perhaps because she'd been disappointed by men in her previous relationships, she couldn't consider that I just might be telling the truth. The last time we ever spoke to each other was an eye-opener for me. During our conversation, she brought up the picture once again. My answer remained the same. But she got hostile, telling me that she would cut me with knives and stick forks in me. And then she had the nerve to ask if I were still coming to meet her. Be very careful about whom you deal with.

I have no idea why a person assumes you have committed a crime, when your main focus is only to help them. A woman named Jane had worked with me for about two years. I never saw her as attractive, even though she had a decent body; she wasn't my type. But that is irrelevant. She and I had a brief conversation about how God wants us to conduct ourselves as Christians. Sometime afterward, Jane called my house, looking for my roommate Alvin; he also worked for the same company. Jane and Alvin had something going on and kept in touch with each another. Alvin had talked about Jane cooking him food and the nights he spent at her home, but he never said he was in love with her. That made it clear to me that they were having an affair. When I told Jane that Alvin wasn't home, we had a conversation about life. I didn't think our phone conversation would lead to a backlash that would blow me away. And the backlash didn't come from Alvin, which made it harder for me to grasp. The next day Alvin asked what Jane and I had talked about, and I told him. I asked Alvin why he wanted to know, and he said Jane had told him I was trying to hit on her. I concluded that she was trying to see how much Alvin cared about her by lying about me, because she suspected Alvin didn't want her as a girlfriend. And the only thing I was trying to do was enlighten her about God, to help her in some way.

Will people ever learn about the true love God has for his people? If only they would take the time to hear him. "Like an earring of gold and an ornament of fine gold, so is a wise reprover upon an obedient ear" (Proverbs 25:12 KJV). If we can hear God speaking to us, then we know how to receive his blessings. One day I was riding in my car, searching for a job, and I was broke worse than shattered glass. I had a good mind to take one road, but on second thought decided to take a different one. Once I took that route, I noticed there were two elderly women whose car had a flat tire. Even though my mind was burdened with the fact that I had no money, I still was able to help someone else. I won't lie, while I was changing their flat tire, I thought it would be nice if they offered me something, but I did not ask them for one red cent. After I had finished, one of the women reached into her purse and gave me a twenty-dollar bill. I was so grateful and thankful. I know that it was God who blessed me, because I was obedient when I heard his soft voice tell me to stop and help those women. If God makes you change direction, your blessing may lie ahead. There are times when you may hear God's voice directing you to go somewhere, and it seems like there's nothing there. But never stop believing, it is a joyful feeling to know that God is taking you to a place more glorious than your current one.

Like many people, I wish pain did not exist. But if it weren't for pain, God could not help us develop the maturity that enables us to cope with everyday life. It was painful to see my mother cry for hours about things that may or may not have concerned me. I remember her telling us that she wouldn't always be with us, and we needed to learn how to do things on our own. I couldn't stand it when she said that; I'm sure I speak for my siblings as well. But she was right. And she always hoped and prayed that she would see all her children grow up. Even though my mother's comment was painful and unwanted, it prepared me for her death. And I was grateful that her prayers were answered and she saw all her children become adults.

When I was a child, I always wanted to stick my head into tight places it didn't belong. That phony voice of Satan, pretending to be the voice of God, convinced me to stick my head between the refrigerator and the wall. It was painful to be stuck in a place where I couldn't free myself by my own power. God tries to teach us to stop putting ourselves into tight spots that can hinder the flow of his blessings. When we continue to sin uncontrollably and fall into trouble, we depend on someone else to bail us out. If we keep striving for God's Word, it will not be so easy for us to get stuck. And the pain that we may encounter might encourage us to get closer to God.

Some people need help to conquer an insecurity that gives them low self-esteem. But after they have overcome this insecurity, they do not recognize the person who helped them during the process. I visited my brother Tony one summer in Albuquerque, New Mexico, while I was on vacation from the army. My brother and I hung out at the gym; his friend was there as well, and both of them worked out tremendously. The first time I had met Tony's friend, he was a very slim man. I could tell that my brother enjoyed helping this guy to build muscles; at that time, my brother was a professional bodybuilder. The next time I went to visit my brother, this same guy was so ripped and toned, I couldn't believe my eyes. I was a bit jealous because I wished it were me. This guy didn't look the same as he had before; his confidence went through the roof. Months passed, and one day Tony told me that this guy had won a trophy from a bodybuilding contest, but not one time did he acknowledge that my brother had helped him. I could hear the disappointment in my brother's voice; maybe he thought this guy could have been his one true friend. And people are your true friends until they use you up; then they go on to the next one. I can't see any logical explanation for forgetting the ones who have helped you climb a ladder that you found impossible to climb on your own. If you aren't careful, you may pass them on your way back down. Most of the time, that's how it happens. Don't use people for your own gain; you never know when you may need their help again.

There was a time when I thought I had a true friend; we played ball together almost every day after school. It wasn't anything from me to walk from my house to his, because it was about one or two miles away. Many times Gary and I played so long, I had to walk home in the dark. And even though I was afraid of the dark, I didn't mind staying late, because I really enjoyed Gary's company. We never got into a fight about anything. We never know what may cause a friendship to end. I don't think we should allow anything to break up a great friendship. But you can't speak for another person because things will test you; a woman or man or money may come between two friends. In this case, I got kept back in the fourth grade, and little did I know that would lead to the end of our friendship, even though we still lived less than two miles apart. But it was obvious that Gary didn't want to be my friend, because I was in a lower grade than he was. He would pass me in school with his new friends and not even look my way. Those years in school without us communicating had a great impact on our friendship. After high school, Gary moved to Florida, and I joined the army; that was the final break that ended our friendship for good. Several times I'd go home to visit and went by Gary's house, but I could never catch up with him.

Oftentimes someone else would speak briefly about Gary. By then, however, I was convinced that our friendship would never be mended and I would never see Gary ever again. But after many years had passed, someone left a message on my answering machine. I didn't recognize his voice, and he didn't leave his name. After a few days passed, this person called back; luckily, I was home to take this call. And after this unknown person had been talking for a while, he told me his name was Gary. I was astonished to hear from him after all those years, and the memories of us playing ball came quickly to the forefront of my mind. Gary told me he was getting married; he invited me, but I wasn't able to make it to his wedding. I was happy for him, though. It takes a real man to examine himself and admit when he is wrong, because Gary said that he realized who his true friends were. I could feel his pain but wasn't sure if we would return to the friendship we once had. Today, Gary and I talk on the phone from time to time, and we once hooked up to play some basketball together—after twenty years. Maybe the way I see friendship is different from others. But I believe that friends shouldn't be apart for years before you hear from them again. If you have a friend who treats you well, remain his friend no matter what. You may not find another like him. Many people say that circumstances and situations change, which is true. But your status as a friend doesn't have to change, unless you allow it to.

I am not the type of person who discriminates against other nationalities. But I get angry when people help their own kind and neglect others. While I was working at Panasonic, the managers were collecting money for a contractor who had to have an operation on his hip. I'd heard that the man, who happened to be white, didn't need any money, because he owned a plane and had money. But you never know who needs what, and that isn't the issue. The managers made sure they didn't forget to ask everyone if we wanted to give. I don't want to sound like a hypocrite because I don't mind helping people, but I can't understand how people who need help don't get it and those who don't need help have it handed to them, even when they don't ask. Here is another reason why I was disturbed by this issue. Another guy, a black man, was standing under one of the gates above the dock doors when one of them accidentally came down on him and damaged his ribs. He was bleeding an excessive amount of blood. This accident put the man out of work for more than two months or so, but not one soul in management asked anyone to contribute. And this man's tragic accident happened way before the contractor's hip operation. If they had no problem helping one man, why not help someone else and not allow race to be the reason for their decision.

People will have no problem standing up for you if you have a good attitude, integrity, and a warm spirit. When I was in the army, my section chief, Sgt. Williams, and I had a pretty good relationship. We made sure respect was present at all times, and I kept in mind that he was my boss. Whatever he wanted me to take care of, I did it with pride and was punctual because he respected me. Sgt. Williams could give me a task and not have to look over my shoulder, because he knew it would be done. One morning, he instructed me to go to the motor pool and get with the mechanics because our field vehicle needed some attention. He wanted me to assist them if they needed help. But when I got down to the motor pool, none of the mechanics had shown up, so I sat around until someone did. The first person to arrive was Sgt. Brown, who ran the shop. No one liked him because he had a nasty attitude toward everyone, especially the guys who had a lower rank. He knew that he could talk to them any kind of way and get away with it. But this day was different; he got to see how it felt to be talked to like a dog.

Sgt. Brown noticed that I was sitting on the right-side front tire of the Humvee. I didn't think it would be a problem or that I could harm the tire just by sitting on it. But Sgt. Brown had something to say; with an angry look on his face, he instructed me to get off. I was a bit disturbed but had no problem doing what he asked me to do. He was an E-5, and I was an E-4; that was enough for me. Later that morning Sgt. Williams sent Spec. Fisher down to the motor pool to help as well, but the rest of the mechanics still had not shown up. Fisher told me that they were in a meeting and that was why they were late. He and I waited several hours for these mechanics to work on the Humvee, sitting around, just shooting the breeze. I realized that Fisher was sitting on the same tire I'd been sitting on earlier. I didn't say anything to him because I didn't think it was a big deal. But then all the mechanics showed up, along with Sgt. Brown, who with his nasty attitude told Fisher to get off the tire. Then Sgt. Brown took his frustration out on me and told me that I should have warned Fisher, because I knew better based on what he'd said earlier. At that point I was angry because Fisher and I had been waiting for them, and he was worried about a tire. Sgt. Brown and I got into a little argument. I made sure that I wasn't insubordinate, because I knew I had to respect his rank, even though I didn't respect him as a man. Sgt. Brown repeated why we shouldn't sit on the tire; then he said that I could leave. As I walked away, I said out loud that I would get Sgt. Williams. Sgt. Brown didn't like that at all.

Race wasn't much of an issue in the army as far as I could tell. I'm not saying that discrimination didn't exist, but a man's rank measured his authority: the greater your rank, the greater your authority. I felt in this case, there was some racism on Sgt. Brown's part, or he was just a grumpy guy. He was an E-5 and he was white, but Sgt. Williams was black and was an E-7. It was obvious that meant something, because when I said I would get Sgt. Williams, Sgt. Brown called me back into his office and commanded me to stand at parade rest for a long time, while he talked to me about gibberish. I think he didn't like the fact that a black man had the power to get in his junk and he wouldn't be able to respond the way he really wanted to. While I stood there in the parade-rest position, which didn't feel like rest at all to me, I was furious. Tears began to run down my face because I really wanted to put my hands around his neck. I felt like a wild beast waiting to be unleashed. There was nothing I had done to deserve this shameful treatment. Fisher must have felt my pain and called my chief, because before I knew it, Sgt. Williams was walking into the office. Boy was I glad to see him. I'm not saying he was God, but he was my protector, and that day he protected me from the big bad wolf. In a loud voice, Sgt. Williams asked, "What the hell is going on here?" Sgt. Brown tried to lie about me, but Sgt. Williams didn't buy it. Once Sgt. Williams began to go off on Sgt. Brown, Sgt. Brown then insisted that I leave, but Sgt. Williams demanded that I stay. I was glad that the tables had turned. Sgt. Williams told Sgt. Brown that he'd told me to come to the motor pool, and he knew that I would be there. Sgt. Williams was so angry, he told them to fix the vehicle on their own without any assistance from his driver. I didn't look at this incident as a racial issue, meaning that I was not glad to see a black man chewing out a white man. I was glad that someone who had more rank came to my defense. For God to come to our defense, our attitudes must reflect his leadership.

When I worked at Panasonic, I had a great discussion with a coworker about the various changes that life brings. I said, "Life is something else," and he commented, "Life is hard, and there are no instructions." My response was plain and clear. I told him that we do have instructions; God has made sure of that. The reason we ignore those instructions is because we insist on fixing things on our own. For instance, we will purchase an item but will not take the time to follow the steps to construct it, clear in our minds how we think it should be. We use that same mentality to fix our lives, but we cannot ignore the fact that God has given us instructions to live. "The fear of the Lord is the beginning of knowledge: but fools despise wisdom and instruction. My sons, hear the instruction of the father, and forsake not the law of thy mother" (Proverbs 1:7–8 KJV). If God instructs a son to listen to his parents, then don't you think God's instructions should have greater prominence?

Many of you who are reading this book may hate your lives because of what you are facing, but if you do something productive, life will get better. Don't do anything to make matters worse. I had a brother-in-law named Greg who was in the navy. He would come home to visit and take me for a ride in his glistening red car. I enjoyed the times he'd throw the football back and forth with me. I also thought that he had some dignity about himself because his appearance stayed fresh. He seemed happy the times he came home to visit, because he always kept a smile on his face. I never expected that he would do something to create a mess for his life; but I was only a kid. As I got older, I found out that Greg wanted to get caught smoking marijuana in order to get discharged from the navy. Afterward his life spiraled downward. Greg's thoughtless decision cost him his wife and kids. Even though I was not a grown man, I felt the pressure that both my sister and Greg were under. And there were hardly any jobs around to support a family in the town in which we lived.

Once my sister and Greg got into a big argument, and my older brother and I went over there to see what was going on. The word was that Greg had put his hand on our sister. When my brother and I got there, my brother wanted to beat Greg up. But when my brother began to swing at him, Greg pulled out a gun, which made my brother pause. Later we found out that the gun was not loaded and did not have a firing pin, but just the thought of him pulling out a gun was bad enough. I also felt that if he could hit my sister, then he should have taken a beating like a man. But my main point is that Greg made a very bad decision. We face many adversities, and we want to take the easy way out. But that way may not be so easy in the long run. Every time you want to throw it all away, simply project your thoughts into the future, and know if you do right, right will do you.

This next story is about someone who might have given up on life, but she didn't. I was watching television one day, and a talk-show host was talking to a woman who didn't have any arms. She'd lost them in a bad accident. Her mother was on the show as well; she told the audience that her daughter would cry all the time when she was younger, but she had to learn how to do for herself. The mother said that over the years as she kept encouraging her daughter, she adapted to the fact that she had no arms. She didn't let that stop her from being active. The host showed a clip of this woman using her feet to drive and to pick up her baby. It seemed as if the baby knew something was different about his mom, because all she had to do was to lean toward him, and he would cling to her. This lady wanted to live; she did not feel sorry for herself despite her handicap. She inspired me to deal with my problems better, and I also realized that though most of us have all our limbs and senses, we still complain about every little thing. We have no right to complain. So even though you may feel out of place, stay on course, even if it means doing what you don't want to in some cases.

# CHAPTER 7

# Circus Tree

Water is there to quench our thirst, but a fire can scare you, depending on its uncontrollable blazing flames. And it will make any lazy person move. One Sunday morning at church, the pastor asked me to pray. But the words in my heart wouldn't come out of my mouth, which caused me to stutter a few times, but I kept praying. Afterward, I felt I had failed. When I got home, I was still discouraged; I flopped down on the couch and didn't want to move. But I noticed that my roommate Steve was cooking something on the stove. He was in his room, but I didn't pay too much attention, because Steve would check on it. I went and lay down on the couch.

Suddenly, I felt that something strange was going on in the kitchen. I quickly jumped off the couch and ran to see what was happening. The pan was filled with grease and was on fire. It wasn't the first time that Steve had left the stove on, but one of us had always caught it before the pan was engulfed in flames. I believe this fire was showing me that my faith in God was inconsistent; because I had stumbled over my prayer, I thought God wasn't there for me. And that was selfish of me, and God knew what he was doing.

Well, that fire made Steve and me move like we had a purpose in life. Steve said he was sorry; I told him it was meant to happen. Sometimes it takes something like a fire to move us from one place to another, and with a sense of urgency. I don't know what fire will force you to move, but don't walk away from it. Contain it, because walking away will only spread it and do more damage. If I allowed myself to feel defeated after I had prayed in a way I thought was pitiful, that spark could have lit a fire that turned me into ashes. Don't beat yourself up because it seems like your best isn't your best. If you have to pour a little water on the flames, so be it.

You never know where your light may shine; if it is bright enough, it may shine into the darkness where others reside. One of my coworkers, whose nickname was Ten, asked me to go to his home and talk to some of his friends about God. When I arrived, I found out that it was his wife who wanted me to come. I had talked to Ten several times at work, and I had no idea that he was sharing our conversations with his wife. It was a blessing to know that someone wanted to hear my opinions and thoughts about life, that there is not many ways to live it, but the Lord's way, if you take it from my perspective. Evidently, those conversations I had with Ten traveled into the lives of others, and they yearned for more knowledge. I am not the only man who understands how God works, but I am the only man who knows how God deals with me, and I can share that with others. That alone can be a powerful lesson and tool for leverage. And that I can explain better than anyone else, because it's my life and we do share some of the same attributes that can ultimately persuade us to live a life according to God's will.

There were several other people at Ten's house. It is difficult to comfort a loved one after you have learned this new way of life, which is very difficult to commit to. While I was standing near Ten's kitchen, one of his friends asked me a question that puzzled me. And I had to get this man to understand that we need to take what is useful to us and throw the rest of it away. His question was, "How can my uncle tell me how to live my life, when my uncle's life is not suitable for a grown man, even though he is a preacher?" I will not make excuses for this preacher, but a preacher is still a man and that will never change. This guy was confused because his uncle told him to live a certain way but did the total opposite. He asked me the question once more. I said,

> Does it anger you? You can't worry about what you can't change in others, but use those things they say that are right, which can be very helpful. We look at what people do, and if they are not doing what we think is right, then there is nothing they can say or do that will help us. The Bible clearly speaks about taking the plank out of your

own eye before trying to take the speck from someone else's. And just because a person has a plank doesn't mean he is without righteousness. You will not reach that next level if you are simpleminded.

After I left Ten's apartment, I hoped that he, his wife, and his friends had gotten something out of my visit and would not let the plank in my eye dictate and determine how they lived for God. I hoped a sprinkle of light had splattered on them, which is all it takes to brighten any darkness, no matter how thick it is.

The Holy Spirit is a powerful entity and knows when someone is going through something. It doesn't need your help to access this information, but it needs a voice to encourage others that everything is in the Lord's hands. One day I was riding past a coworker with whom I hardly ever held a conversation. This guy looked like he was never happy; I hardly ever saw him with a smile on his face. On this particular day, he had dropped some wide-screen televisions because he was in a rush as he pulled a large order. I restacked the televisions, forgetting the fact that we'd never talked. I believe in teamwork to get a job done; we both worked in the same place and that made us a team. Just before I finished restacking them, he pulled up to help out. I felt in my spirit that God wanted me to assure this man that God knows all things. I asked if he believed in God. He replied yes, and I asked how his marriage was. We talked for a little while, and he said he would return later to continue our conversation. About twenty minutes later, he called me over and asked why I asked him about his personal life. I told him that the Holy Spirit could feel his pain; I was just following directions. Now, I had not known anything about this man or his relationship, so I was astonished when my roommate Anthony told me that the guy had mentioned some things about his relationship. I know this man probably thought Anthony told me his business, but God revealed it to me and knew that his spirit was in distress. Many people fake their happiness; they put on masks and take them off when no one else is around. They say to themselves, "I am too hard to let anyone know how I really feel about my life." Holding things in and telling yourselves that everything is all right will get you nowhere. Talk to someone who can understand what you are facing because you can't relinquish those feelings alone. You need help from the Spirit of God. Think of the Spirit as a ventilator shaft that allows fresh air to come into a coal mine; invite the Spirit into your hearts and receive its fresh charity.

Some people may not live up to the standard of God's cleanliness, but we as Christians must bring joy and a positive attitude to the less fortunate. A woman named Mrs. Dickson who stayed in our neighborhood had a good heart. But we couldn't see this woman as a woman of God because of an odor she carried around with her everywhere she went. The odor hid the fact that she was a nice woman. Call me crazy, but people are judgmental, and most of the time we can't see beyond what we think we know. My mother had a heart big as an ocean, and she didn't allow Mrs. Dickson's uncleanliness to get in the way of God's love. She insisted that Mrs. Dickson and her granddaughter spend a few days with us because her husband had passed away. At that time I didn't understand why because my mother was a clean person. Having Mrs. Dickson and her granddaughter's stench in our home, I don't believe any other person would have done what my mother did for them. And I am grateful for my mother's courage and love, because it taught me how to judge and not who to judge. "Do not judge according to appearance, but judge with righteous judgment" (John 7:24 KJV). Since I have been traveling on this predestined journey, I have learned many things, things that I didn't understand in the past. I know now that God was with this Mrs. Dickson. It didn't matter what she was or wasn't able to do; she worked with what she had. God was her protector. Several times Mrs. Dickson found snakes in her old wooden home. But she had some dramatic encounters with those snakes, and God always prompted her to spot them first. Once I walked by her house, and she was outside, putting a snake in the fire. Most people would have cut off its head or shot it, and that would be the end of it. But not Mrs. Dickson; she made sure that that snake would never see daylight again. So if you think a person is not in the will of God, think again and be careful about how you judge them. You may not be in his will!

We should apply the same type of dedication God has for us to serving him. His dedication to us never staggers; it paves the way. We, however, lack dedication toward God but have no problem sitting at a football game at below-freezing temperatures until the game is over. When I was in the army, I was dedicated to buying as much music as I could. As soon as I got my paycheck, I went to the PX and bought tapes or CDs. I could never satisfy that urge to have new music. When new music came out, it stimulated my mind; I wanted to have more music than anyone else. Many times I bought as many as ten CDs at one time. I had more than two hundred CDs, which were stolen out of my car. And another time I had collected almost the same amount again, but I had to sell them because I needed the money. That dedication to music did me no good in the long run. But it did remind me to refocus my dedication on something real and not something that lasted only for the moment. We sometimes assume that money grows on trees, based on the way we spend it. At times, we say we'd like to have lots of money, but if you had it, many of us would not know what to do with it. Look back in time; much money has probably circulated through your hands. And most of that money went to waste if you didn't know how to manage it. Having lots of money and no intellect about how to manage it can put you in a worse position than if you had none at all. A strategy will allow you to hold on to that money; plan to save and invest, and stop making stupid mistakes, like paying for the same thing twice.

In 2001, I had a nice, red Suzuki 400 Bandit, for which I'd paid hardly anything. I put the bike in the shop to get the carburetors cleaned. After paying more than $500 to get my bike out of the shop, I finally took it home. Later on in the evening, I knew that it was going to rain, but I didn't cover up the bike because I was too lazy. The next morning I went outside to start my bike, and I had trouble cranking it. But I kept hitting the switch, and it finally started. At that point I had time to make the right choice and cover up the bike, because it wasn't like I knew whether or not it would rain again. The day was pretty clear, with no dark clouds to be seen. However, after the sun went down, my bike was hit again by the rain, a lot worse than the last time. The next day when I tried to crank my bike, it would not start at all. I let the bike sit for two years, until I got tired of it taking up space on the porch. I placed the bike in the shop once again for the exact same reason. Someone from the shop called and asked me to bring in some money before they started doing any repairs. I gathered about $200 initially; but my patience grew thin while waiting to get the remaining part of it, so I decided to leave the bike in the shop. I lost the money I paid to fix the bike twice, plus the money I'd paid for the bike. The Bible tells us how careless we are when it comes to money and that we should be more careful about how we spend it. "Now therefore, thus says the Lord of hosts: consider your ways! You have sown much, and bring in little; you eat, but do not have enough; you drink, but you are not filled with drink; you clothe yourselves, but no one is warm; and he who earns wages, earns wages to put into a bag with holes" (Haggai 1:5–6 NKJV). This is what the Spirit of God tries to teach us: we should not spend money just because we have it, but spend it wisely.

I have always tried to treat people nicely, but every time I did, I got treated like a doormat. And it upsets me when people don't appreciate what someone else does. One day I offered one of my coworkers some gloves. I used to bring these gloves from home and give them to guys at work who I thought were cool. It wasn't like the company supplied us with any work gloves. One guy, to whom I hardly ever talked, said he didn't need any. But the next day he asked me for a pair of gloves. I said, "I offered you a pair yesterday, and you said no, you were straight." Can you believe that this man snapped at me? Then he said that he hadn't needed them the day before because of the job he was doing. Even though he had a nasty attitude, I still gave him a pair. Even people who say they are living for God sometimes don't think about anyone but themselves when their wants and needs have not been met. They don't realize that when they hurt a child of God, they are hurting God. This short-tempered man was a minister. I thought he should have recognized that Satan was influencing him to provoke me. We as Christians should be aware when the devil is trying to use us to get to another person. How can that be from God? We must elevate our way of thinking and strive to think like God.

Failing to keep your word will lead to contention and strife between human beings. And God doesn't like ugliness. Your feelings toward a person who has let us down began changes. For example, during my time in basic training, I got to know a few guys. But I felt that one particular guy, who slept directly across from my bunk, could have been a potential friend, because he and I had some mature conversations about life. However, it didn't take long to find out what type of person he truly was. I decided that I could trust him based on the conversation we'd had. I assumed that he was a mature young man. One day, about noon, it was sunny and mild. We were sitting on a hill, and Mark began to talk about his wife. He wondered if his wife would support his decision to be in the army. Because he opened up to me, I thought he was a cool guy. Perhaps his background and home state, New York, were interesting to me as well, because Georgia was the only thing on my mind. At that time, I had not been anywhere else; I wanted to know what New York was like, and he didn't mind sharing his story with me. One day Mark asked to borrow ten dollars from me; he agreed to repay it once he had received some money from his wife. I had no problem loaning it to him, because I had confidence that he was a friend. What I couldn't understand was why his wife had to send him money—I imagined it would be the other way around—but it wasn't my business to meddle. Without any discomfort, I reached into my wall locker, took out the money, and handed it to him. Mark gave me no reason not to trust him, because he promised me that his word was good.

Some days passed, but Mark never approached me; I assumed his wife hadn't sent him any money. I patiently waited on Mark to meet his obligations. One day we had mail call. Mark went to get his mail and walked back to his bunk with a great smile on his face, so I knew that his wife had sent him some money. I stood near my bunk, waiting eagerly for him to pay back the money that he owed me. Mark didn't say a word to me, and I didn't say anything to him, because I was sure that I wouldn't have to remind a grown man about something he said he would do. And I always feel eerie when I have to hold another man by the hand, if you know what I mean. Anyway, Mark quickly rushed downstairs to call his wife. He was on the phone for about thirty minutes to an hour before he returned to his bunk. When he came back upstairs, I was still cleaning my wall unit. Mark said something to me, which wasn't nice at all. I wasn't sure what was wrong with him, because I knew I hadn't done anything wrong. Before I knew it, Mark accused me of stealing the money his wife just had sent to him. I was shocked and enraged because he owed me money and had avoided me after he got his money. Mark only said that because I hadn't gone downstairs to make a phone call. He suspected me of taking his money. I told Mark, "I didn't have to steal your money, because I have money in my locker." Actually I felt sorry for him, because I knew how he must have felt to have someone take his money. However, it seemed as though his money vanished into thin air, because I didn't see anyone come near his bunk the whole time while I was standing near mine. But if a person is careless with his things, he deserves to lose them.

Later I found out that when Mark went downstairs to call his wife, he left his wall locker unsecured. And I wasn't the only person who knew he had received money; the person who took it probably watched Mark the whole time. I could be wrong, but I believe that if Mark had done the right thing by paying me back, this probably wouldn't have happened to him. What goes around comes around.

Take care of your friends, and your friends—if they are true—will take care of you. If you are a leader, you can't allow your so-called friend to hinder you from leading. While in basic training in December 1992, I was made a squad leader because our former squad leader had been discharged. I didn't want this position, which came with responsibilities that I wasn't ready to take on. But I didn't want to turn it down either, because I didn't want my colleagues to think I was a wimp. Not only that, I thought I had to take it because my drill sergeant had snatched the badge off the former squad leader and thrown it directly at my chest. At first, I didn't know what to do, because I had never been in charge of anything. But I knew that being a control freak wasn't an option. I also felt like it wouldn't last long because of what had happened to the previous guy. I wondered what caused the sergeant to revoke his position. But I said I would do my best, and my best may not have been good enough for the drill sergeant. This was a leader's position; once I left basic training and got to my permanent duty station, I already would be prepared if I wanted to become a leader in the real army.

During the time I was acting squad leader, I enjoyed the position very much, because I had privileges other soldiers didn't. But, like I said before, I knew it wouldn't last. I knew that my friend Vick and I would bump heads. Vick didn't like anyone telling him to do anything, but he knew that it was important to do what the drill sergeant said. If the drill sergeant gave us a task, how would I handle it? Sure enough, the day arrived when the sergeant wanted my squad to clean the floors; every Friday some squad had to clean a certain area in the barracks. I knew I would have a problem getting Vick to help out. This guy in whom I confided on a day-to-day basis, and who I thought was a friend, sat on his bunk that day and did nothing while everybody else worked. I felt the pressure right then and I saw the ending even before the drill sergeant had said one word to me. And I knew that someone from the squad would say something, because I didn't use my position as being a leader. I believed if this guy was a true friend, then I shouldn't have had to say anything to him; he should have been glad to help out. I was appalled at the way things went down when I was in charge. I can remember it like it was yesterday, the day I lost my crown. Drill Sergeant Plant was built and tough. He called me into his office and asked me why I didn't say anything to Vick about sitting on his bed and doing nothing. I stood there speechless. And just as quickly as Sergeant Plant had given me that badge, he snatched it off. That day had a great effect on me, because once I arrived at my permanent duty station, I didn't want to be in charge of any personnel. I made sure that I wouldn't get in trouble for someone else's stupidity. Once the sergeant took the badge, like I said, I was speechless and relieved at the same time, because I knew that would be the last time I'd get embarrassed about something so childish. And I didn't have much to say to my so-called friend. But if the shoe had been on the other foot, my friend would not have had to ask me to help the squad; we were a team. The Bible tells us, "Faithful are the wounds of a friend; but the kisses of an enemy are deceitful" (Proverbs 27:6 KJV). Back then, I couldn't see the significance in being a leader. But I know now that you must separate business, friends, and pleasure.

Some people are prone to mess things up for everyone else. I am not saying I am perfect, but I have no problem thinking about others first. Consider how someone else may feel before you make a crazy decision. While I was in basic training, we were in the cold field for a weeklong training exercise called bivouac. While we were in the field, the snow began to fall very heavily, making the day even worse. About thirty soldiers had to sleep in a large tent. If my memory serves me correctly, there were only two heaters, one on either end, and not everyone could gather around it at one time. One particular night, after we went to bed, some guys were talking pretty loudly. I could feel something deep in the bowels of my belly telling me that we'd be in for a treat before the night was over. The loud talking went on for quite some time, until the drill sergeant got fed up. He came into the tent and told them to be quiet. I was hoping that the sergeant wouldn't do anything outrageous, because they had no problem making a soldier do some crazy things, like taking all the bunks outside. One drill sergeant told a soldier to hold a dummy round that weighed more than ninety pounds or so for about an hour; of course, he ended up dropping it. Our drill sergeant said that if the noise didn't cease, he would come back with authority. As soon as he left, the noise diminished for a moment, but not long after he'd walked out, it was louder than before. I knew it wouldn't be long before the sergeant made his statement a reality. With anger and rage, the sergeant walked into our tent and demanded that everyone get dressed in five minutes and be in formation. Those nuts who had been talking weren't thinking about anyone else but themselves, but everybody had to pay the price. We stood outside in that cold weather; no one went anywhere until the sergeant passed out the mail, and that took about an hour.

Now that I am older and wiser, I think about when I've been selfish, engulfed in my own glory, and was not thinking about the next man. I took advantage of a good person. I worked at this company called Shultz Container, which made plastic containers for several different companies, including Coca-Cola. My shift was at night, a long, twelve-hour shift that lasted from 6:00 p.m. until 6:00 a.m. We all had a set schedule every week—three days on and four days off—and the following week it switched, unless you wanted to work overtime. Anytime I worked overtime, some of us would be outside when we should have been working, but the supervisor didn't say anything to us. I knew that it was wrong, but I didn't consider this supervisor's authority at all. Who knows? We could have messed things up for him, if the word had gotten out that he wasn't doing his job. I considered his position as supervisor, but I also took advantage of it at the same time because he allowed us to. If he had told me that I wasn't being paid to goof off, I would have taken his authority more seriously. Similar situations, but two different outcomes. Consider others because you never know when you'll want someone to think about how you may feel about something. We face many challenges today for this same reason; someone does something stupid and suddenly everyone's windows of opportunity are closed.

You can't rely on man to give you the answer to questions for which only God has a solution. The answer is already contained in you, and it takes a special key to open the lock, which is developed and shaped only by the Holy Spirit. One Wednesday evening while I was in Bible study, a woman asked the pastor, "How are we supposed to keep going when things are constantly being thrown at us by the devil?" She asked this question several times. The next day I kept thinking about why she'd been so determined to ask this question. I even meditated on it while I was at work. It seemed to me that she was looking for an answer from the pastor, the answer would not come. After I had pondered on this incident for quite some time, I felt God would give me a revelation about a mysterious thought this woman had encountered. Acceptance, we must learn to accept things and let the man above do the rest.

When we are out in the world, danger is everywhere around us. We don't worry about anything, though, because we are doing what the world wants us to do. Anytime you expose yourself to the things and the ways of the world it is hard to see the negative effects they have on our lives. How can we be concerned about something that exists when we can't see it or feel it? But when we are touched by God, he makes those things visible so that we can sense when we sin against him and we can tell when we are invalid. We worry more when we are close to God than when we are out in the world doing everything we want. And that isn't God intent, he shows us these things to be aware of them. God will not put more on us than we can bare, even though it may feel that way at times. In fact, he draws closer to us when we reach out closer to him, and the more we reach out, the closer he comes. God is in control, and I can prove it based on things that have happened in my life.

I got caught up in something that set my life back, further back than I wanted to go, but God allowed me to look toward the future. I never imagined that believing in God would make me so focused. I don't worry about things that I can't control. And I stay on top of those things that I can control. I don't see people as enemies anymore; I see them as people who don't know God. My thoughts of righteousness are like a double-edged sword; if I cut someone else down, I realize I am cutting myself as well. I say what I mean and mean what I say—most of the time. I have learned many things from my belief in God, but most important is the will he has given me to want him more than anything in this world.

Be careful about who you associate yourself with, because it is easy as one, two, three for you to be drowned in their mess, simply because you hang with them. It would be nice if people took a chance on God and sought his righteousness. He can give you the discernment that will help you determine which people will help you improve yourself and not drag you down in the dirt. While I was working at Panasonic, some new guys came to work. They were temps but worked full days. Three of these gentlemen were friends, and they played every day like kids. I talked with one of them, Jeff, from time to time. Many times we wish people we care for can see things the way we do and how they will work out. Anyway, Jeff and I were standing near the time clock with one of Jeff's friends and a few other people who were waiting to clock out. Jeff's friend was the first one at the clock; he raised his foot up, pretending he was going to kick the time clock, but then accidently kicked it and knocked it off the wall. But when the word got out, some people said that all three guys were playing around, including Jeff. I knew, of course, that only one guy had caused this accident. It is very important to know who you are dealing with at all times. You never know what others may do to get you into trouble, and without your consent. It was difficult for Jeff to get away from his crew because he had to clock out. But in some cases you have to separate yourself from your crew, period, if you want to be a part of the transformation of the body of Christ.

And some of the smallest decisions we make can be stifling, and suffocate the life right out of us. There was a time when my name was included in a situation I didn't have a whole lot to do with, but it was a decision I had made which brought this upon myself. When I was in basic training, I and some other soldiers were standing out on the pad one evening. We noticed the pizza guy bringing someone an order. During that phase of basic, we weren't allowed to order pizza. But a few guys got bold and took a chance one night. They asked if I wanted to chip in, but I said no. In that situation, I made the correct decision. But once they ordered the pizza and took it in the barracks, however, it was very tempting. As they went into the large shower room to eat the pizza—and to hide the evidence from everyone else—my friend asked me if I wanted a piece. I did, but I wasn't sure if I wanted what would come after it. I took a very small piece of sausage, thinking that I could not get in trouble for that. Boy, was I wrong. The next morning we were all in trouble, and not one of the guys stood up for me. The drill sergeants had us doing all kinds of crazy things—pushups, rolling over like a dog, flutter kicks—for about a month or two. On top of that, they gave us an Article 15 (i.e., punishment without a court-martial). I was so angry at myself, because I knew eating a slice of pizza was wrong. I didn't think that eating a piece of meat would have that much impact. Whenever God pours his blessings upon you, never relax, because it doesn't take much to mess it up. It is a responsibility, so you must take care of it, if you want it to take care of you. I had a supervisor who was very young, between twenty-three and twenty-five, for his position, but qualified and very intelligent. I know that it was hard for him to be a young black man with that position. However, the more I got to know him, the more I felt it wouldn't be long before he would lose his job. For one, he began missing days like he was just an ordinary worker. Don't get me wrong; everyone takes a day off from time to time. But when you are in a certain position, you cannot miss days for any old reason, like staying home with your girl and smoking weed. A leader has to check on things regularly so that operations continue. Eventually, the young man was fired for not doing his job.

Some of the stories I share with you must be heaven-sent; the story I just told you must have come directly from God himself. I say that because the night after I wrote this story, my nephew called me on my cell phone. I didn't want to answer it because I was getting ready for Bible study. Suddenly, he called the house phone. I planned to call him back later, but then I thought that it could be an emergency and picked up. My nephew asked, "Do you remember Wendell who used to work at Shultz Container?" I told him, "Vaguely." My nephew had run into Wendell at the gas station. He wasn't the young man who lost his job, but he'd worked at the same company. I felt that was more than a coincidence. During our walks with God, he leaves trails to guide us down the right path. But we can't get there if we don't do the work.

Many people walking the streets are stranded because they don't have a car. And some Christian people hear directly from God to give a person a ride or to help someone, but they won't, for whatever reason. I am not saying that you must pick up every person that is walking, because a lot of crazy ones are roaming the streets. What I am saying is that God touches our hearts when the time arrives to pick up that certain person or help those stranded on the road. We can't be afraid of what might happen, especially when God has laid it on your heart. Use your discretion to judge each situation; for example, a woman must be careful about picking up a man. And men may worry about how many people to pick up at one time. But the most important thing is to open up our hearts a little more to receive even more of God's glory and love for others.

I was traveling back to my hometown one weekend to take care of some important matters. There were two routes I could have taken to my destination: ride through the town of Dublin or stay on the interstate and get off at the exit leading to my town. My first thought was to take the exit at Dublin, but it was only a thought, nothing more and nothing less. But suddenly, out of nowhere, as I came upon Dublin's exit, the decision was made for me to get off. Usually when I went home, I took the other route. I did not know why I took that exit, but I felt in my heart that reason came from God and he would show it to me as I kept driving. I drove about four miles down the road and saw some people pushing their car off the highway. I immediately turned around to help them. One gentleman told me they had run out of gas. I took them to the store to get some. This all took place around 10:00 p.m., but I knew it was a divine plan from God. One of them told me that no one else had stopped to help them.

And there was another time I was en route to my hometown. It was in the evening, right before the sun went down. I passed an elderly man walking, and was compelled in my heart to stop and pick him up. But once I stopped along the road and waited for him to get to my car, I wanted to change my mind and leave well enough alone. I tried to think of another way to help him without allowing him to get into my car, because I was a bit apprehensive. I didn't know what he was capable of. But when he reached my passenger-side door and I could see him clearly, I asked where he was headed. He said Florida. I relinquished those thoughts of negativity and gave him a ride. After he got into my car, I told him that it is very dangerous to pick up strangers. For some reason, he made me feel at ease, maybe because he didn't try anything stupid, and we just talked about life. We told each other our names. He told me the reason he left Michigan. He had been hanging around people who were doing drugs, and that encouraged him to do them as well. He had quit and moved in with someone else, but he said that wasn't good enough; he had to leave it all behind. I believe that he left people he may have loved very much just to find peace. But sometimes it takes a bold move to get yourself on track. As we kept talking, his conversation got even more personal. He told me that his wife had left him with only fifty cents, not dollars but cents.

Despite everything he was going through, he still declared that God was taking care of him and said that he refused to lie down and die. Those encouraging words strengthened my faith. If this man, who didn't have anywhere to go or anyone he could call on, could keep holding on, then what could I say for myself, whose situation was far better. Sometimes people who are stranded need more than a ride; they just need someone to talk to.

When you let a person know that he is doing something that displeases you, it may lead to a great friendship, depending on how that person values you. When I was stationed at Fort Stuart, in Hinesville, Georgia, I met a guy whose last name was Powe. I arrived at Fort Stuart about a week before he did. I found him to be a pretty cool guy. I asked Powe if he wanted to take a ride one evening with my cousin and me; his response was yes. We rode around for a while into another town and stopped at McDonald's to eat. I paid for Powe's meal, because he didn't have any money at the time, and he said he would repay me. I would have bought his food anyway; but the fact of the matter was that he said he would pay me back. I expected him to do so once he had some money. But Powe seemed to forget that he owed me until one day he needed my help, and I brought the debt to his attention.

Powe asked me to follow him as he dropped off his car at the shop; he said he would give me something for gas. And that was when I told him how I felt about the last incident. I didn't care if I lost a friend. I needed to get my point across, because if you don't let people know how you feel, they will take advantage of you. "Powe," I said, "if you tell me you are going to do something, then do it, because I was kind enough to do what you asked of me." Then I reminded him about the previous time he'd said he would repay my money. I also told Powe that I'd rather he not tell me anything about paying me back, if his word wasn't good. From that point on I had no more problems with Powe. We had mutual respect for one another, and we were close friends until we went in different directions in the military. Powe reenlisted and went to Korea for a year, and we lost communication. I assumed I would never see the guy again.

I get puzzled when things happen out of the blue. A year later, I happened to go to the PX, which is a military store for the enlisted and everyone connected with the US Armed Forces. As I walked around in the store, I ran into Powe. We were glad to see each other, and our friendship was the same as before he had left. Don't be afraid to let people know how you feel about things; it can help them to become better people and better friends. And it will close those cracks that give the enemy an opening to play how he wants, as long as he wants, and whenever he wants.

# CHAPTER 8

# Marlboro Tree

An incident made me wonder why getting gray hair is such a big deal. If we live long enough in this world, the odds are very great that we will automatically get gray hair, and there is no need to complain when it appears. One day I called Elaine, to whom I hadn't talked with in a while. After we greeted one another, Elaine said she had gray hair. I gasped with a little smirk, but I didn't mean anything harsh and didn't think it would hurt her feelings. But it obviously did hurt her, and she let me know it, telling me, "That damn mess isn't funny." I felt she needed an apology to smooth things out, because my intention wasn't to cause any harm. And out of nowhere Elaine began crying; I asked her why she was crying. But I knew what the problem was, even though she didn't respond. She really didn't have a reason to cry, especially when there was nothing she could do to stop this process of attaining gray hair. My thoughts were that we complain about too many things that can't help us get into the kingdom of God. I have sympathy for Elaine and all people who feel they are getting too old and haven't done anything with their lives. They believe the beauty they once had is gone forever, never to return again. I say to those people, "It is a blessing to get gray hair as you strive to the things of God." Proverbs 16:31–33 (NKJV) tells us:

> The silver-haired head is a crown of glory, if it is found in the way of righteousness. He who is slow to anger is better than the mighty, And he who rules his spirit than he that takes a city. The lot is cast into the lap; but its every decision is from the Lord.

I understand that both the wicked and the righteous get gray hair; but God makes it clear that the ones who live right get the crown of life. I assume this means that you have endured the trials and tribulations that come along with living. And a man who rules his spirit, and thus has control over the things that want to control him, is mightier than a man who rules a city. God places quite a bit into the lap of man, but the final decision is his. We may find ourselves doing that very thing we have avoided doing for many years, only because God has made us. We are the puppets, and he is the puppet master.

God has revealed to me that I have many preconceptions about events before they occur. I hope to motivate and compel your minds to a higher level in God. This knowledge leads to less worry because, in due time, God will prevail. In life, people despise leeches that refuse to let go once they are attached. But in this case, forget all the bad things associated with being a leech; be a leech and latch onto God. I know that it is easier said than done, I struggle every day with my faith in God, but I will not ever allow myself to let go. It is stated in the Bible: let go of those things that easily beset us.

We must be observers to see where God wants us to end up. One night my friend Charles and I went out to eat at a sports bar. A man sitting directly across from us at the bar was talking to a lady who was sitting between the guy and us. For some reason, he asked Charles if he was traveling. We didn't understand what he meant by that. The word *traveling* stuck out like a sore thumb to me, because before we went out to eat I had written about an incident dealing with that word. I found it exciting and fascinating to know that God was traveling my way and showing me that my book would be manifested in the future. Actually, the man had used the word *traveling* as a code for something else. He wanted to know if Charles had any weed. When I was in the army we used codes, so that when we went to war the enemy wouldn't know what was being said. God gives us many ways to decode the secrets that will allow us to reach our ultimate blessing he has waiting for us.

If you are eager to get married, and wear a wedding ring and are not married, the ring will not have a sentimental value or represent a promise between two people. But wearing a band without being married can still contain high principles. This was brought to my attention by my friend Charles, who promised God that he would wear a band and not have sex until he was married. I could understand why Charles thought God would be pleased with him. But I would have to think twice about wearing it for any other reason. Suppose you are an unmarried woman wearing a wedding ring who goes into a restaurant, where you enjoy the food and scenery. Your eyes meet a man's, and you feel there is some chemistry. He might want to talk to you, but the ring on your finger sets off an alarm. The only way he might approach you is if he doesn't care if you are married and just wants to sow his wild oats. Some women wear wedding bands to keep men from stepping up to them, but if you think that that will keep all those vultures from attacking you, you are sadly mistaken. In fact, you may even attract more your way, and then what? I believe in my heart and in my soul that women who try to hide themselves behind a ring are afraid that the right man may come along. They may even feel they are unable to be virtuous for any man, who knows. Or they might feel shameful that they are not married. I know I might get a whole lot of flak about this issue.

I bring it up because I've seen a woman with a wedding band in church, although I knew that she wasn't married. For several Sundays, I noticed this nice-looking and bright young woman, who came in right before the pastor began to preach. Once I asked her if she wanted to go out to dinner, but she didn't take me up on my offer, which was all good with me. On one particular Sunday, I, as a minister, was sitting with the pastor in the pulpit as she entered the church. As she went to sit down, I could see a wedding band on her finger. And I said to myself that she must have taken that step toward marriage and looked away for five minutes or so. She was a nice catch, so I turned my focus back on her, and saw her switching rings. Many of you will say that was her prerogative, and this is true. But it made me wonder why anyone would go through the trouble to make others think one thing when she knows good and well that it is something else. I am open to suggestions, because I want an understanding about why people do this. Don't take this the wrong way; all I am saying is don't turn a lie into the truth and the truth into a lie. I also hope that virtuous woman marry a God-fearing man.

In everything you do, strive to mean what you say, and say what you mean. Make your meaning plain, because you don't want to look like a fool if you tell someone one thing and then come back with something different. For example, when I was at Fort Bragg, I did not close my hood all the way, and it popped up as I was driving one day and cracked my windshield. I called several junkyards until I found a windshield I could afford. I asked my neighbor, Jesse, if he would give me a ride to pick it up. Once we arrived at the junkyard, Jesse asked if I needed his help to take the windshield from the junked car. You should never turn down help unless you are certain that you can handle things on your own. I was a bit skeptical about taking his help, because I thought if he cracked it, would he pay me back my money and I couldn't be mad because I let him help. But I did indeed need his help, so I gave him a screwdriver. The very thing I hoped would not happen did happen. As Jesse tried to pry the windshield out with the screwdriver, it cracked. I was very disappointed, but I didn't get mad because it was my fault as well. I was surprised when Jesse offered to pay for the windshield. He felt obligated to take full responsibility, but I said he only had to pay half. When we had arrived back in our neighborhood, he asked if I were sure, because it wasn't a problem for him to pay the whole amount.

I don't know why I didn't take Jesse up on his offer, because it was his fault. But I blamed myself as well; if I hadn't allowed him to help, Jesse would have been out of the picture, and everything would have been on me. I had the chance to get all my money back, but I was too messed up in the head to simply say, "Yes, I want all my money." The problem was that Jesse was a pretty cool guy; I enjoyed talking with him from time to time, and I didn't want to lose him as a friend. That can be a problem for many people who don't want to be honest with a person, fearful of running them off. Anyway, a couple of days passed, and I walked over to Jesse's house and asked if he would pay me the other half of the money. I'd had several chances to get all the money, and I should have taken it when he offered it. I felt really stupid when he told me he wouldn't give it to me because I'd had a chance, and he was right. That taught me a valuable lesson about meaning what I say and saying what I mean.

I don't always understand my own feelings. But my feelings empower me to keep going, no matter what obstacles I face. My motivation increases when I don't feel like being motivated. Of course Satan is there, trying to hold on to my tail to keep me from reaching my maximum potential. People you think are friends will say things about you. I met Diane at my job; she planned to help me with this book, but it didn't work out. I thought she was a pretty cool person, because she told me that Dan had told her I was weird. Dan was a coworker, and I thought he was a nice guy. We talked several times out of the day, and I thought we would become friends one day. I considered what Diane said and wondered why Dan said I was weird. But he would tell me about calling different women even though he was married. Dan must have thought I was weird, because I didn't act like him and I didn't think the way he did. I was, and still am to this day, only striving to remain focused on a task that was placed in my lap by God. But sometime the heart gets in the way, which can be a burden when we want to understand life. "Therefore my spirit is overwhelmed within me; my heart within me is distressed" (Psalm 143:4 NKJV). When our hearts feel empty due to those things we don't understand, we have the spirit as a backup to bring our hearts joy. You don't have to walk around with a sad face when you are degraded by people you thought were your friends. Words are very powerful, powerful enough to hinder you from moving forward and at the same time powerful enough to exceed you. We must use the tactics God has given us to fight back at the enemy and gain liberty. And those tactics that edify the spirit of the Lord dwell in his children once we gain his knowledge.

> Do not love the world or the things in the world. It simply saying that anyone who loves this world more than God, then the love of God is not in them. For all that is in the world the lust of the flesh, the lust of the eyes, and the pride of life is not of the Father but is of the world. And the world is passing away, and the lust of it; but he who does the will of God abides forever. (1 John 2:15–17 NKJV)

> Death and life are in the power of the tongue, and those who love it will eat its fruits. (Proverbs 18:21 NKJV)

> Yet in all these things we are more than conquerors through Him who loves us. For I am persuaded neither death nor life, nor angels, nor principalities, nor powers, nor things present, nor things to come. Nor height, nor depth, nor any other created thing, shall be able to

separate us from the Love of God which is in Christ Jesus
our Lord. (Romans 8:37–39 NKJV)

If someone doesn't expose the wicked people of this world, especially
when they don't mind exposing themselves, how are we to survive? I
understand that in some cities, towns, and hoods this would be called
snitching, but to tell on one to protect many more takes a lot of bravery.
I have no problem with this, because if they are caught, they deserve
what they get. We need one another's help to stop the enemy from taking
whatever he wants.

When I was stationed at Fort Bragg, I lived in a trailer park owned by
a sweet, elderly African American woman. She had about eight trailers on
her land, which was located in Springfield, North Carolina, a small town
near the base. When I was in the field, that trailer seemed like my favorite
spot. During one particular field exercise, which lasted longer than any
of the previous ones, I got a message from my section chief that the door
at my house was wide open. I knew I hadn't left it open. I dreaded the
thought that someone had broken into my place and stolen what little that
I had. They rushed me in from the field, and I arrived at my house. The
door was wide open. And everything of value was gone. It was a hard pill
to swallow, but I had no choice except to allow it to slide down my throat
as if I were taking some bad-tasting medicine. Later a neighbor told me
she saw the two men who broke into my home carrying my things out the
front door. I couldn't believe what I was hearing; I thought I was in the
twilight zone. What she said sounded crazy. Why didn't she call the cops?
It wasn't a bad neighborhood where snitches who talked might get killed.
As this woman was telling me who had broken into my place, I found out
that one of the men stayed in the neighborhood. I'd even let him come over
once or twice, because I thought he was pretty cool. He'd told me that he
worked at the military store as a barber. And I let down my guard, because
I was careful about the kind of people I allowed into my home. But once
I did, he saw what I had, and from that moment his mind was set to steal
from me. He just had to wait for the right time.

I am aware that there are places in our nation where people's lives are
just terrible. In some neighborhoods, if you see someone doing something
wrong, you keep your mouth closed. Otherwise something bad could

happen to you. Still, money can do only so much for a person, but that is another subject. I am referring to knowledge, wisdom, and instruction, things your kids can have once they understand the art of living. People who know their purpose and have love in their heart must be the bridles that restrain the wicked. We must be brave enough to take on this task; future lives depend on it. Many of us are passive and think that we should keep quiet when we see the enemy in action, but God said to fear no man. You can't be afraid of the one that can kill the body, but you must be afraid of the one that can destroy body and soul. I am not here to convince you to tell every bad thing you see, we have to be led by the Spirit of God and filter out what to tell. Nevertheless, as children of God, there are some things which we must not become involved in. We may not be strong enough to handle the aftermath. In other words, we must be equipped with the Word of God, which prepares our minds, bodies, and souls to deal with the consequences that may occur when we help someone else. You must have some of God's traits to have love for others and to stand strong against the wicked.

I give God thanks for showing me many signs and wonders and helping me to understand them after he unleashed them in my life. Some wonders are there to give me joy, and others are there to keep me motivated. At work one day, Edmond and I were unloading a truck stocked with two types of products. One set of items were flat-screen televisions, which sat on the floor of the truck, and the other items were the television stands on top of the televisions. I told Edmond taking off the stands first would make it easier for us to get to the televisions. He agreed, but I repeatedly had to bend down, crawl on top of the televisions, retrieve the stands, and take them to the rear of the trailer, where Edmond stacked them on pallets. I wanted to stop because it felt like each one was heavier than the one before and my back was hurting. But I kept going. I wanted to get it over with as soon as possible. I finally reached the front of the trailer and the two remaining stands. As I picked one up, I noticed that there were two different types of stands, and these were lighter than the others. I had to share with others the signs and wonder what I got from this incident.

When life gets hard and the pressure seems unbearable, don't quit. If you train yourself to endure and keep pushing, things have to change, even things you can't change on your own. With the will of God, they will change with time. That is something that we must accept: we need God to be the head of our lives. If Satan can blur our minds and alter our thoughts from God, we will always think that life is too hard to live. Don't forget about the times when you have fallen flat on your face and were able to get up. God encourages us to get up over and over again. No matter how many times you fall, you can get back up, and it can be better than the last time. Practice makes perfect.

How can we have a better society when we ignore an issue raised by another human being? One day at Panasonic I had to use the restroom; there was another guy in there as well. While we were using the restroom, the cleaning lady entered without even announcing herself. The other gentleman had gotten off the toilet right before she barged in the door. I mentioned this incident to a supervisor, hoping to get some results. Almost every Monday morning we had a company meeting to discuss the plan for the week and what was expected of us. The assistant manager usually started the meeting, and it ended with the warehouse manager. During one meeting, after about ten minutes or so, the assistant manager said, "When the cleaning lady is in the restroom, do not go in." I was confused about the whole thing; he'd turned the story around. Then one coworker asked, "What do we do when she walks in on us?" But no response was given. From that point until the time everybody was laid off, no one tried to resolve the problem. We must make other people's opinions matter, because that will make a better society. And we should take action when problems arrive and listen to what people have to say, instead of being evasive and avoiding answering the question at hand. It would be nice if we could be honest, whether or not we can help. Many people would appreciate honesty more than hearing nothing at all. Last but not least, we must show and give respect, from the smallest to the greatest. Just because you are in a high position, don't think that a forklift driver's opinion is a waste.

God is always aware of what is going on in your life, and he will let you know through signs or dreams. One day I was excited about going to Bible study; I'd also been fasting the same day. I'd made up my mind that I would not eat anything until the service was over. But when I got home from work that evening, I had a change of heart. My lights were off, because I was having some financial difficulties. That upset me, and I broke my fast. It almost kept me from going to church that evening as well.

But I went anyway. Once I arrived at church, I felt that I wasn't dressed for the service. Everyone else was dressed for a revival, and I was dressed casually. I had gotten my dates mixed up. I wanted to go home and change my clothes, but I knew if I went home, I wouldn't return. I realized that I would be allowing my flesh to control my actions, just as I had done when I broke my fast.

But that next morning I had a dream that strengthened my spirit and soul and confirmed that God knows. In this dream, I had no gas rather than no lights. My brother called me, saying I could come by his house if I needed to stay warm. I asked myself how he knew I had no gas. Not long after I awoke that morning, my phone rang; it was my brother. He asked me something that only I'd known about, and I asked myself how he knew. It was breathtaking the way that God appeared to me, letting me know that he knew what I was dealing with.

How can you make a decision by assuming that a situation happened? It is hardly likely to succeed unless you know all the details. You must probe from the beginning to the end, because the person you say is guilty may be innocent. When I was in the fourth grade, my friend Tim and I got in trouble because of two white girls. We had left one class and were entering into Mrs. Durden's class, and once we walked in her class, she wanted us to calm the noise immediately so we could get straight to work. Mrs. Durden was writing on the blackboard while everyone was sitting at his or her desk. It didn't seem like she was paying attention, because she was too busy putting our work on the board. As she was writing, Tracy and Michelle said something funny to make Tim laugh, and I laughed as well. Tim's laughs became louder and louder, and he made the teacher turn around. I tried to keep mine under wraps, because I didn't want to get into trouble, but I knew trouble was coming whether I wanted it or not. Every time Mrs. Durden faced us, we quickly stopped laughing, and as soon as she turned her back, the laughing began all over again. The final time, we thought she wasn't paying attention, but she caught Tim red-handed. And she punished both of us by taking away our recess; we loved going outside to play. Instead, she made us write the same sentence about three hundred times. In her mind, I guess it was impossible that the white girls would make us laugh or cut up in class. Mrs. Durden didn't ask what the problem was or who was causing it; she pointed her finger at Tim and me and made us the culprits. I was troubled by the way she concluded that Tim and I had interrupted her class. But what else could we do but accept it; in her mind she knew that she was right, that two little black boys were the troublemakers.

We as human beings can come together after a big disaster confronts us. But as soon as things simmer down, we fall into that same rut: killing, stealing, hate, etc. When 9/11 hit, people drew together as if the world were coming to an end. It had nothing to do with being black or white, rich or poor. Something had been shattered, and everyone pulled together to diminish the pain. For something like that to happen again, we have to learn how to control the anger or rage that resides in us. And that can't happen unless we have the love of God in our hearts. And that will start with one person saying, "I can live by God's commandments." I still have hope that a massive group of people can unite with love. But it must start with each of us saying, "God is my fortress, my shield, and my witness, and I will exemplify his love." I know that I am not the only one who thinks that something of this caliber can be done. It would be a sight to see, if it were real without the wrong intentions or motives.

Many of us have pessimistic thoughts when it comes to a task we need to complete or learn. But the story I am about to share with you doesn't require that much effort. It only takes one person to start a change, if he trusts in God and endures the pain that is entrusted to him or just having determination and a desire to want it. No pain, no gain. About three weeks into basic training, our drill instructor demonstrated how to perform a functions check on a M60 machine gun. This action is done after you have fired your rifle for a certain amount of time, and it gets hot and stops firing. It looked easy while the drill instructor was on deck; we were young and did not realize that he had been doing this for many years and could probably do it with his eyes closed. When it was my turn, I told myself that I would never learn the sequences, because it looked so difficult; it was like life, in a sense. But I knew I had to learn this task to graduate from basic training and move on with my life.

One day the instructor brought the gun to the barracks, so we could practice more. Some guys took the opportunity, and some were too afraid; others thought it would be a breeze. I was one of the guys who defeated the negative thoughts and took advantage of the opportunity, because we didn't know how long we'd have the gun to practice. When I first started, I slowly went through the steps. Before I knew it, I was one of the fastest guys in my platoon. And earlier I had said to myself that it was impossible, but nothing is too hard for God. With God on his side, one man can believe that his mission is possible. But for change to happen, we need his love, will, and power. Sitting around will not get the job done. "The Lord rewarded me according to my righteousness; according to the cleanness of my hands, he has recompensed me. For I have kept the ways of the Lord, and have not wickedly departed from my God" (2 Samuel 22:21–22 KJV).

There isn't nearly as much police brutality now as there has been in the past. I definitely give all the praises to God that he has minimized this injustice. But racism still exists today, although these days they try to provoke us, so we will get belligerent, and they can throw us in jail. It is called racial profiling. One way of profiling is to think that every black man who has nice shiny rims on his car is a drug dealer, and the police pull him over for no reason.

One Saturday, after I got off from work, I went straight home and changed clothes to go out on the town. I admit I was looking pretty fresh. Anyway, as soon as I pulled out from my apartment and onto the main highway, there was a police car on my left side. I tried very hard not to assume that this cop wasn't like the majority of them. This time was different; my car did not have flashy rims that would make me seem like a drug dealer. We drove side by side for only a few minutes before he turned off to his left. Once I realized he had fallen back and wasn't driving behind me, I said to myself that he wasn't like most of them. I focused on something more important. But then I happened to glance into my rearview mirror, and there he was driving behind my car. Thank God I had all the documents it takes to drive a vehicle. I feel like my opinions about this issue are correct, and I know that many black men will agree. I am aware not all white people are racist. But some can't seem to grasp that we too are people, and we deserve respect. We are not beasts in the wilderness.

Can you recall the incident from April 2006 when a security guard thought that a black congresswoman was an intruder? My research tells me that this was described as a racial event. She was accused of entering the building without her identifying lapel pin and failing to stop when asked. But representatives are not required to go through metal detectors when they enter and leave the building. Several police sources said the officer, who was not identified, asked her to stop three times. When she kept going, he placed a hand on her, and she hit him, according to the officials. Some people said the officer did not recognize her and grabbed her because she was black. I wondered how you could mistake a member of Congress for an intruder. Evidently the security was not that secure since anyone could walk into the high profile Capitol Building. "The tents of robbers prosper and they that provoke God are secure; into whose hand God bringeth abundantly" (Job 12:6 NKJV). I thank God for all those in the past who have faced racial brutality on all levels that our race might be physically free. Now it is up to all races to be free in their minds through the will of God. This congresswoman was secure in her profession and knew that God had her back. And she had every right to act the way she did. I wonder if we will ever overcome racism. We shouldn't have to wait until God unleashes his wrath upon us before we learn how to extract this evil entity from the earth.

One Sunday evening after church, my friend Charles and I were talking about how everyone needs to be on the same accord with God. But many people have their own agendas, even after they confess that God is their Lord and Savior. And I believe that keeps God from moving the way he would love to move in his children's lives. Charles said, "God will not bless no mess." It was poetic, concise, and meaningful at the same time. I told Charles, "A house divided against itself will fall." Once I got back home, I decided to spend some quality time with God, because I wanted to hear a word from him. We may go to Bible study, Sunday school, and the Sunday service and feel that is all we need. Maybe some of us believe we don't have to maintain our love for God anywhere else. Anyway, once I got home, I got on my knees and prayed to God. Sometimes you have to encourage yourself to remain on your knees. I know how difficult it is at times to pray to someone you can't see or hear. After praying, I picked up my Bible, not planning to read anything in particular. The book just happened to open to the book of Matthew, specifically to Matthew 12:25 (NKJV): "But Jesus knew their thoughts and said to them: Every kingdom divided against itself is brought to desolation, and every city or house divided against itself will not stand." If that wasn't a word from God assuring me that I was in tune with his ways, then I must be crazy. When you build your house, make sure the foundation has the imprint of God.

Playing with something that should be taken seriously can have a bad result. While I was stationed in Fort Bragg, my friend Hill and I were headed out from the barracks. We made a left onto Bragg Boulevard, the main street that went through town. But Hill and I were traveling the opposite way. It was raining, and once we made this left I felt the rear end of my car slide just a bit. I didn't take it too seriously, because if I had, I would not have accelerated. I wondered what would happen if I tapped on the pedal just a little while it was sliding. I wasn't going more than thirty miles per hour once I made the left. Before I knew what had happened, my car had hydroplaned, and I lost control of the steering wheel. If I remember correctly, my car spiraled about three times in the road and then went into the ditch. The accident damaged my car pretty bad, and I had to pay out a lot of money to get it fixed. My point is, don't think for one minute that your life is safe if you do not take it seriously. Just as easily as I had this accident, I could have avoided it. I knew that my rear tires were slick, but I didn't think before I hit the gas pedal. All I had to do was slow down the first time I felt my car sliding.

We all live and learn, but I believe that learning first and then living can be rewarding. We Christians are drawn to people who aren't Christian, which can be both helpful to and bad for you; it all depends on how you deal with the situation. After I gave my life to God, I thought about something that had taken place in the past; I was a bad influence on a friend. In the army I met a nice guy whose last name was Jones. I had known Jones for quite some time, and he did not mind if I went to his room after physical training to take a shower and change into my fatigues for our 9:00 a.m. formation. I stayed off-post, and it didn't make any sense for me to make the drive. But before Jones and I became friends, I would hear other guys say nasty things about him, such as that he had an ugly attitude. And that was because Jones spoke his mind and he didn't let anyone run over him. Some people don't like when someone stands up for himself. That didn't matter to me because he gave me respect. And he didn't do a lot of crazy things, unlike some of the other guys, who would lose their whole checks in one night from playing dice and running around with all types of women. Jones was conservative and a Christian, and I had no problem associating with him. But I wasn't a Christian at that time, and here is where the issue lies.

I asked Jones if he wanted to ride to Albuquerque, New Mexico, with me to visit one of my brothers. He was thrilled about the trip. After we had arrived and settled in, we met up with a young lady that I had met on a previous visit to my brother. I told Jones that she had a friend as well. We took the young ladies into town for pizza. Jones and the young lady must have had feelings for each other, because at the end of the night, they kissed. As we headed back to my brother's house, I tried to persuade Jones to have sex with her, because that was where my mind was. The next day was Tuesday; Jones and I had firm plans of leaving that Thursday. But the two young ladies wanted us to stay until Friday, so we changed our plans. We were all thinking about having sex. The two young ladies said they would call us Friday morning and tell us where to pick them up. But God will intervene when Satan tries to tempt one of his children. It wasn't like I wanted to harm Jones in any way, but Satan was using me as bait in order to get to Jones. I had no idea that I was a small fish being used to catch a bigger fish. Jones was a Christian, and Satan wanted to stick his fork into him. Finally the long-awaited Friday arrived; Jones and I sat around, waiting for them to call. Around noon the phone rang; we weren't too quick to answer it, because we didn't want to seem too anxious and eager. Seconds before I picked it up, my brother walked in and said, "Don't answer my phone." All the other days Jones and I had been at my brother's house, he had been at work. I know this was an indication that God wanted Jones to keep his commandments, remain strong, and not to allow friend or foe to deceive him. And I was that foe, acting as a friend.

## CHAPTER 9

# A Tree that Owns Itself

Have you ever been in a conversation with a person and, out of the blue, someone else interrupts as if you weren't even there? This second person may claim to be a Christian. How can we grow if we don't use the manners our parents taught us and achieve a level of maturity that considers and respects others? Once I was in a conversation with a coworker, and all of a sudden a woman who worked in the office barged into our conversation and showed him pictures of her daughter's wedding. They once worked together in a different department and knew each other pretty well. But that didn't give her the right to drop into our conversation. What made it worse was that she didn't say excuse me.

One day, I was talking to two gentlemen about a well-known bishop that was under scrutiny. A white woman entered the lobby where we were. She overheard our conversation but not everything, and she asked, "What happened?" No one had been talking to her or had said one word to her. Many people are so disrespectful. I think manners reflect whom we serve. For some, this is like a dog that tries to catch its tail but never succeeds, because they have no clue about what I am saying.

It is hard for people to believe that two individuals of the opposite sex can't have a simple friendship. Often in the workplace a man and a woman get acquainted with one another and do not want to take it further. But everyone else assumes they are more than friends. I used to speak to a nice, full-figured woman who worked in the office. Once I saw that she was a down-to-earth person, I wanted to get to know her even better. I hoped she could help me retype my book; maybe we could have helped each other out. I went out of my way to greet her by walking into the office. One day I thought it was the right moment to ask if she would help with my project. She agreed to help, so I talked to her even more, because we were working on something that hopefully would benefit us both. We dedicated ourselves so much to this project, someone thought we were having a fling. My friend said that someone had asked him if this woman and I were having sex. If only that person had a mind like God's so he could see beyond his natural sight or had asked if we were a couple, I know we both would have told the truth. But then people would have asked if we were lying or not. They were so narrow-minded, they didn't have the ability to see through clear glass. And why worry about what others may be doing? Such activity is like a tornado that can't be controlled once it has reached its maximum potential; it will destroy everything in its path. In a way, that is how Satan uses his powers, by using others to tear down someone who is striving every day to live a positive life.

Deputation is a group of people who speak on the behalf of others. That doesn't mean that everybody has to say something; it only takes one to represent everyone else. Once I was taking a computer class, and halfway through, we got a new instructor. Mr. Hensley was a white man in his forties, and he knew a lot about those computers. Not long after he began the class, he invited his six black male students to breakfast, but only five showed up. As we entered the restaurant, we noticed a black couple arguing. The male was doing most of the talking; I could tell the woman felt belittled, and I believe that everyone else felt the same way. I was astonished by what happened next. Mr. Hensley, in a nice tone of voice, told the guy that he shouldn't talk to her that way. The man told Mr. Hensley, "Mind your own business." I was in awe, and I am pretty sure my colleagues were as amazed as I was. And I believe Mr. Hensley spoke for the group, because no one disagreed with his actions. And the black gentleman he was confronting wasn't small; he was tall and muscular. Even though I thought he should have stayed out of it, Mr. Hensley was speaking for us as well, because the man was disrespecting the woman in many ways. Right in the entrance, he was cursing her like she was nothing. And I know that if we weren't there, the situation probably would have happened in a different way. Mr. Hensley most likely would have walked right past the couple and entered the restaurant. He had some balls, because I wasn't planning on saying anything and the others guys probably weren't either. Who knows how things would have turned out if this man had jumped Mr. Hensley? Afterward, we black guys never discussed how we felt about it. But I was glad that Mr. Hensley spoke his mind, even though he may have believed we would protect him. That was cool with me, because he did the right thing.

My love for God is so great. He has given me the ability to foretell that something will take place and that I should share his love with someone who truly needs a change in their life. When I go to a place I have never been before, I believe that God wants me to reconnect a soul to him. One Saturday a friend and I were riding and checking out several different stores, looking for some reasonably priced, back-to-school clothes for our sons. And we found a store where we were happy with the prices. As I was walking to the checkout counter, I noticed a lady with whom I had once worked with. I couldn't tell you how long it had been since I'd last seen her. But after we greeted one another, she told me about all the bad things that were going on in her life: her friend wrecked her car, and she'd lost her job. I thought that was my cue to talk to her about God, and I was eager to share his truth. I knew that God wanted me to be at that store and at that particular time. I had prepared myself as I pulled into the parking lot, because I felt that something would take place. Also, I had never been in the store before, although I had passed it many different times.

Not long after I met that lady, I stumbled upon another former coworker while I was out eating with my brother and a friend. I asked the young man how he was doing, and he said he was just out because he didn't feel like cooking. This proved to me that meeting the lady was no fluke; God's plan was in place, and he was waiting for me to complete it. Sometimes we feel when unusual things happen that someone else may think we are crazy to even have such thoughts. But if we don't stand for something, we will fall for anything. I can't tell you how to live or what thoughts to think. But I will say, hold on to the love of God through it all.

There should be a law against people who don't know how to bridle their own tongues. It should be a crime for someone to degenerate another human being, for example to criticize someone for being overweight. If people are not trapped by their weight, and do not have low self-esteem because of it, and are proud of who they are, then let them be. I had a classmate named Sherry who was not an enormous girl, but she did carry some weight. I thought that she carried it very well, but some of the other girls disagreed. I'm pretty sure Sherry heard many fat jokes during her time in school. I could tell that she had a competitive will to rise above all the harsh things that were said about her over the years. But it is crazy how life bites you in the butt. Some years ago I went to a funeral of a close friend and neighbor who had passed away. His funeral was at the school auditorium, where I saw Sherry again several years after we graduated. She stood there with her arms folded and a glow around her body. As we waited outside for the eulogy to start, Sherry told me the ones who called her fat in school were now bigger than she was. What a twist!

While I was listening to Sherry, I remembered an incident from my army days. I'd felt demoralized by a girl who one of my friends was dating. Stevens had mentioned this girl to me several different times. The way he talked about her, I pictured a fascinating woman. When the day came for me to meet her, I was excited because I hoped Stevens had found the one. Late in the evening, Stevens, two other friends, and I pulled up at his girlfriend's house. We exited the car, all curious to see how she looked. We had entered her house, and Stevens introduced everyone to her. Then everyone sat down, except me, because there was nowhere for me to sit. Some time passed, and I could tell that for some reason she didn't like me. I sensed this the first time I walked into the house, because she said something to me that I didn't like, and we exchanged a few words. I had to stand up for myself, and it didn't matter to me if she were female or male, I didn't say anything bad to her, so she didn't have to degrade me the way she did. After that incident, I thought it was all over, but I guess speaking my mind made her even madder. She had the nerve to call me "yuck mouth," and that really made me angry. It made me so mad, I had to walk out of her house; I sat in the car until the others came out. At one point, she asked one of the guys to come get me. I didn't feel welcome, and I didn't want to be in her presence ever again. I won't lie; I hate the way two of my teeth protrude from my mouth. But that doesn't give her the right to degrade me. Not one time did I disrespect her.

Many of you may be thinking about what you might have done if you were in my shoes. But I am not the type of person who feeds off revenge. Even though what she said hurt really bad, I didn't want to stoop to her level. Many of years passed, and I wondered why I was the only one in the group she picked on. One day I concluded that she'd wanted to keep the focus from herself because she was a bit overweight. But as far as I know, no one went there to bash her. If you know you have a flaw that is visible, before you talk about someone else's flaw, make sure you are ready to hear some harsh things about yourself. You never know when you may meet a person who has no problem giving you what you deserve, whether or not you can take it.

> ... that you may become blameless and harmless, the sons of God, without rebuke, in the midst of a crooked and perverse nation among whom you shine as lights in the world. (Philippians 2:15 NKJV)

> ... who will also confirm you to the end, that you may be blameless in the day of our Lord Jesus Christ. (1 Corinthians 1:8 NKJV)

God holds us without blame; but that doesn't keep men from wanting to blame someone else for their faults. And God has a reason for not blaming us, if we allow this passage to dwell in our hearts: 1 John 1:9 (KJV) says, "if we confess our sins, he is faithful and just to forgive us our sins and to cleanse us from all unrighteousness." We need to learn how to be honest with him and confess our faults, so that then we can accept those faults and not blame someone else. I am stressing the word *blame*, and many people don't want to take responsibility for their own actions. I once had a friend who wanted to place the blame with myself and another friend. He didn't care who, as long as it wasn't him who was falling for it. Finley, Ben, and I were all riding in the same car. The car belonged to Finley's mom, who was very cautious when she allowed Finley with her car. After all, we were becoming grown men. Finley's mom let him use the car on occasion. One day we were traveling the back roads to the next town, which was about eleven miles away. Finley was driving, Ben was sitting on the passenger side, and I was sitting behind Ben. I noticed that Finley was driving about ten or fifteen miles over the speed limit. I can't recall if Ben or I brought up the issue, but we did know that Finley had gotten a ticket before because he'd told us about it. I didn't say anything, because I thought he had everything under control and he knew what he was doing. But then we passed a policeman, and he turned around with his lights flashing. Finley began to panic; if he'd had a seat that could eject him from that car, he wouldn't have thought twice about pushing the button. He wanted Ben to switch seats with him while the car was in motion and started removing himself from the driver's seat. Once he saw Ben wouldn't take the blame for him, he asked me. I know he was scared and wondered what his mom would say. But I also felt that he didn't respect our friendship at all if he'd try to pull a stunt like that. He was so theatrical and dramatic, I wanted to take the blame for him, because it seemed that once his mother found out, it would be a major problem. But I knew that wouldn't be the right thing to do, because once you are the scapegoat for others, they will try you again and again, until they have drained you of your dignity. I hope that you don't take the blame for others, no matter who they might be. The Son of the Living God has taken the blame for all of us and he doesn't need anyone to take his place.

Has a dream influenced your way of thinking? God can communicate with us through dreams that appear to be real. I was employed by a company that distributes electronics all over the United States. Employees were told in a meeting that once a year the company would have a competition that consisted of driving a forklift through an obstacle course. But managers would pick the contestants, because the winners would have the chance to compete at the headquarters for all the distribution centers. I was one of the guys who was picked because I drove the forklift pretty well. The competition took place on a Monday, and on Thursday they were to announce the winners. After it was over, I wasn't too concerned about whether or not I had won. I only enjoyed the activities that went along with competition. But I still wanted to do my best, because I am a very competitive person, and I don't like to let someone else win that easy. On Tuesday morning, while I was lying in bed, I had a dream that I was one of the winners, but it wasn't clear if I were first, second, or third. I was stunned, because it is weird to be in an event and then dream about being a winner. I didn't know what to think, so I sat back to see how things would play out. Thursday came, and they announced the first-place winner, who was my roommate at the time. The next name they called was mine. Even though I didn't win first place, I still was a winner, and my dream had told the story beforehand. That led me to believe in God even more. You and I can be winners even when we don't think we are, as long as we keep striving and pressing toward his mark. The first-place winner won a $100 gift card to Walmart, and the two runners-up only received a small trophy. We need not focus our thoughts on material possessions but only on the fact that the two runners-up had something that represented they were winners. And I was glad to be one of the winners, even though my prize wasn't that valuable to the naked eye. But in many different ways it was more valuable, because I did something even faster and efficient than the next person to win, and I was proud of myself. Remember that a winner inherits the will to fight and accepts the fact that he may lose a battle, but he will not quit until he wins the war. And there are many different winners, but only one teaches others to become winners of souls. "The fruit of the righteous is a tree of life, and he who wins souls is wise" (Proverbs 11:30 NKJV).

Having fear in your heart about something that you love doing makes you subject to strongholds that are under Satan's control and will change your way of thinking and your path of life. For instance, my older sister Elizabeth shared a story with me about our mother, who allowed evil to set in and made her afraid to do something she enjoyed. Our mother loved styling other women's hair, and she made some money at it as well. One time a woman wanted to get her hair done because she had a very important meeting to attend the following day. Our mother refused and told her to make an appointment like everyone else. The woman didn't like our mother's response. She became angry and irrational and demanded that our mother fix her hair; if she didn't, she would turn her in, because our mother didn't have a license. Fear crept in and destroyed our mother's joy at making other women feel good about themselves. A tip, be careful and don't let anyone steal your joy. Do what you need to do by getting certified, if that is the case, so that you don't have to worry about someone taking away what you enjoy doing.

Have you ever asked, what is love? Many people have a very slight idea, and then there are those who decline to show it. Some years ago I had a conversation with a guy about the idea of love. I didn't understand his concept of love, but I had no problem sharing what I thought love was all about. He didn't want a woman to tell him she loved him. I told him that many people don't understand how to love, and I thought he was one of them. He replied that love shouldn't hurt. Right then, I knew what his problem was and why he felt that way. But I had to ask him, "Why is it that God can love us and yet sometimes we still hurt?" He said, "God's love is unconditional," and that is a very true statement.

The love that God has given me to share with others yearns inside of me, waiting to be birthed like a baby approaching its ninth month in the womb. If God can love us unconditionally, and we strive to be like him, then we should strive to do the same. One of the reasons why this is so difficult is that some of us have been hurt so bad we don't know how to love anymore and maybe don't want to be loved ever again. After everything this guy and I talked about, he still said that I was wrong. While you are wrapped up in love, there will be hurt. That pain is there to teach us and direct us to a love that conquers all boundaries of imperfection. What is love to you? Is it a parasite that latches onto your heart and eats your soul? Or is it a harmony that cannot be played by any instrument? If we apply ourselves and put the time in, love will happen. It may start out small, but it can grow into something large.

> Another parable he put forth to them, saying, "The kingdom of heaven is like a mustard seed, which a man took and sowed in his field, which indeed is the least of all the seeds; but when it is grown it is greater than the herbs and becomes a tree, so that the birds of the air come and nest in it branches." (Matthew 13:31–32 NKJV)

> And let us consider one another to provoke unto love and to good works. (Hebrews 10:24 KJV)

You need me, and I need you. If we try harder, we can conquer the hate that exists among the races and allow love to reign.

I can definitely identify what isn't love. The love I had for myself was tarnished by my lust for a woman. I blame myself for this because if I hadn't eaten this fruit, things may have gone a different way. But there was no way to escape this trap, especially when I was controlled and led by my own flesh. Young men, take heed of what I say because I have experienced this firsthand: a one-night stand with a strange woman. Be very careful. Many women will take you on a ride like you have never been on before and make you never want to ride it again, unless you want to remain ignorant.

> My son, attend unto my wisdom, and bow thine ear to my understanding: That thou mayest regard discretion, and that thy lips may keep knowledge. For the lips of a strange woman drop as a honeycomb, and her mouth is smoother than oil. But her end is bitter as wormwood, sharp as a two-edged sword. Her feet go down to death; her steps take hold on hell. Lest thou shouldest ponder the path of life, her ways are movable, unstable that thou canst not know them. Hear me now therefore, O ye children, and depart not from the words of my mouth. Remove thy way far from her, and come not nigh the door of her house: Lest thou give thine honor unto others, and thy years unto the cruel. (Proverbs 5:1–9 KJV)

This message is for all men who are ignorant when it comes to pretty women, who have a look of innocence. However, if you are not cautious, they can scare you for life without having any remorse. I became a statistic by having a one-night stand with a strange woman. I now have a deeper revelation, which is that men have been obtrusive to women. It began when my sister-in-law, Nancy, told me about a former associate, Mindy, who would surface at times and contact her out of the blue. I gathered that she was a mysterious woman. Nancy also revealed that Mindy had moved to Washington, DC, but was born and raised in North Carolina. And when Nancy told me about this woman, I was still in the army and I had only two years before I got out, without any blemishes or strikes on my record. It was clean as a whistle. But that would change once I deceived myself by thinking if I kissed her lips, she would no longer be a stranger. How shallow minded of me, that very moment I was already trapped, and predestined to be eaten by a predator, and I would become a predecessor for others. My sister-in-law told me that she could get in touch with Mindy if I wanted to talk to her. Nancy said Mindy was a nice-looking woman, very light-skinned, just the way I liked them. With this information, my mind was already in disarray, even though I had not seen or spoken one word to Mindy. But Nancy also warned me that Mindy was a strange woman. I asked what made her strange, but she never clarified, although she did say that Mindy had been abused by several different men. I assumed that was one of the reasons why Nancy said Mindy was strange. I really didn't think the thing through and decided to overlook what Nancy shared with me. But when a woman tells you something about another woman, you may want to take it into consideration. I don't know how long it took Nancy to tell Mindy about me, but Mindy and I were talking on the phone by mid-1996. And I will share with you how crazy and bizarre my dealings with this woman were.

Once Mindy and I began calling one another, every conversation got longer and longer. I felt like something was there; I just didn't quite know what it was, or maybe it was my other head conjuring up thoughts for me to think that there was something good happening between us. During one of our conversations, Mindy told me that she had two sons. I felt that her calling was a bit obsessive, more than was needed, because of the fact that she had two children to take care of. And that was a thought that lingered many times on my mind. At times we would talk for four hours, and sometimes more than that. There were times I'd try to get off the phone, because I was thinking about her well-being, but she told me it was all right. Some of you may say I didn't try hard enough. I won't lie; I did enjoy talking with her about whatever was on our minds. But the phone calls became redundant. I suggested that she didn't have to call me that much, but she ignored me. During one of our conversations, I got bold and asked Mindy to send me a pair of her underwear, not thinking that she would. She did, along with a picture. Hey, we were just being young and flirtatious, and when she agreed to my suggestion, I think it made Mindy that much more interesting. And that was a spark for me, which made me more eager to meet this sexy woman. What a way of determining who is the best fit for us. I had no idea that her beautiful looks would take me to a place where my life would be like a helicopter spinning out of control. It would take the hand of God to systematically analyze and meticulously organize my mind so that my life could be finalized for his purpose and will.

When Mindy and I were talking one night, she said something that caught my attention, but I overlooked it. Mindy said that if someone tried to screw her over, she would get back at them, no matter what it took. My lust for her overpowered any knowledge I had of seeing the true meaning of her statement. I was vulnerable, and I became a mark. But I had no idea that I would be a victim, because I couldn't see myself doing anything wrong to her; I was a good guy. At least in my eyes, I could do no wrong to anyone. It got to a point when Mindy would call and question me: "Why didn't I call her the way she called me?" I told her I didn't have money like that and I thought her calling was abnormal. Mindy then asked if I wanted her calling card number; I replied no. She was very persistent, but I always said no. One particular morning, Mindy called me earlier than any other time she had called. When I picked up the phone, she asked me to write down a long set of numbers. I was still somewhat asleep, so I didn't know what the numbers were, nor did I care at the time. But after I wrote them down, she said, "These are the numbers to my calling card," and added that I could call her anytime.

Now why do people disrespect your decision? Instead, they barge into your territory without considering how you may think or feel. And while I had Mindy's card, I used it once or twice and called her. What was I to do? I guess I wasn't strong enough not to use it, but I wish I had been, because it would be used against me. As time moved on, Mindy and I grew somewhat closer; we even planned to go with my brother and his wife to New Orleans, where they host a festival once a year. In fact, Mindy asked if I wanted to go, but I wasn't able to go or take Mindy because I didn't have the money. It would have cost about $400 for Mindy and me to tag along. I was eager to go because that would have given me the opportunity to meet Mindy. And the sexual things she talked about doing to me made things even more complicated and exciting. She wanted to pay for both of us, but there was no way I could have let her do something like, especially since I knew she had kids. I wasn't sure what state her mind was in, but I knew it wasn't the right thing to do. She even mentioned to my brother that she would have "mad" sex with me in the van if we traveled with them. During those five or six months we talked on the phone, Mindy had been trying to get in touch with me, and when she couldn't reach me, she called my brother's house. Tony said she was upset just because she couldn't reach me. She said he knew where I was but wouldn't tell her, but that wasn't the case. Tony immediately sensed there was something strange about Mindy and warned me to leave this woman alone. But it was too late; my lust for her was burning and had taken me to a place where there was no return. I had to get even closer to her, and that was the only way to obliterate my passion for her.

After that incident, I had a conversation with her over the phone. Mindy stated that it was easy for her to get pregnant. At the time, I disregarded it and wasn't concerned about getting her pregnant. My plan was not giving this woman a baby. I barely knew her. Although, I knew it was a 50-50 chance of it happening. For some strange reason, I wanted to prove to my brother that he was wrong about this woman. But how can you say a person is wrong when they already have gained some insight about a situation. I am aware that we like to prove others to be wrong, but sometimes that is not the proper tactic to use. In doing so, it creates a vortex, which have your life spinning faster than what you want it to.

Mindy and I remained in contact despite the warning my brother gave me. Our conversation about sex started from the time we got on the phone until the time we got off. Around the end of 1996 and the beginning of 1997, we got tired of talking; we both wanted to see what was at the end of the rainbow. We decided to meet in North Carolina, a place with which we were both familiar. February 27, 1997, is a date I will never forget, even when I am old and gray, because it changed my life from good to bad and from bad back to good. Mindy and I turned up the heat we had for each other by meeting, which later melted and destroyed any hope of us being a couple. Once that day came, I arrived at the motel earlier in the day, and she arrived in the wee hours of the morning, around 3:00 a.m. But while I was waiting for her, I realized I'd forgotten the condoms I'd purchased earlier that day. I decided I didn't need them, because I had a solid plan. And I was too lazy to go to my car to retrieve them. Before I could finish arguing with myself about the condoms, I heard a knock at the door; it was too late to go outside. It was showtime! And I was ready to perform. I knew right then it was going down. By then my mind was somewhere else. I was lost in the world of beauty. Mindy was standing there in an all-black leather outfit; she looked like an enhanced version of a Klondike bar or a York peppermint patty, which give you the sensation where you are in reality; it doesn't compare where you are mentally. She was looking so good that I was oblivious to the spikes of a cactus that covered her body! Not long after Mindy entered the room and lay down on the bed with me, we started kissing right away. That was followed by heated and nonstop sex; we were like a freight-train engine that is full of coal. It can travel for miles, and you never know where it will stop. The first time I reached the sexual peak, I retracted myself from inside her beautiful body, thinking that would keep her from getting pregnant. Nevertheless, I have known it to work on several occasions during my time in the military. The next time it happened, she told me to remain inside her. It seemed as though my mind was gone and I couldn't judge what call to make. My plan was disintegrated, and I became a fool for lust. Her lips were like drops of a honeycomb and her mouth was smoother than oil.

But a week later Mindy told me that she was pregnant. And there was a great chance this child was mine, because I didn't use any protection. Mindy said she wanted an abortion, and I was fine with her decision. She said she would pay half, and I agreed to pay the other half. Without any hesitation or questions, I sent her my half of what she said the abortion would cost. She then told me that her phone bill was unbearably high, I even sent her a hundred dollars extra to help pay it, even though I only used her calling card twice. I thought I was being fair, but she wanted me to be more than fair. The lies and manipulation had begun, and I knew that the fun was over. I was in a pit. After a couple of weeks, Mindy called and said I needed to send her more money, because she couldn't gather her half. That really made me angry. I told her I wouldn't send her anything else unless she provided proof that she was pregnant. After that, Mindy's calls came in like a flood every day; most of them I didn't answer. But on the few occasions I did answer, I told her to stop harassing me. One time she called pretending to be her mother, but I knew it was her. This woman's brain was either fried or nonexistent. I thought back to what my brother had told me: do not mess with this girl.

One time Mindy called, and my friend Marlin was over. While Mindy and I were on the phone, Marlin had made a statement, and Mindy heard him. She wanted Marlin to get on the phone. I knew it was a bad idea, but she insisted that I give him the phone. They exchanged a few words; then she said something to annoy Marlin, and he called her a bitch. Mindy had the nerve to tell me she would come down and slap both of us in the mouth, and why I didn't take up for her. Over a period of time, I thought this matter was done. A year had passed. One afternoon, my colleague and I were cleaning our weapons, and my platoon sergeant called me into his office. I had a good idea that Mindy was responsible for this meeting. Sergeant White gave me a brown envelope, which contained a letter that stated I'd given Mindy syphilis and papers saying I had to show up in court. She was suing me for $5,000 for her phone bill, although I only used her card once or twice. But when I went to court, Mindy didn't show, and the judge threw the case out. I was glad about that, but that was minor compared to what was coming. It was a sharp razor that would separate my belief on what was love and what was lust.

In the past, Mindy and I had exchanged things. I sent her a pair of my fatigues and a set of my ID tags. And yes, I was careless to send my ID tags with my SSN to a person I barely knew. She said she wanted them, and I thought it was harmless. About a month after we began to have a dispute, I got a letter from Mindy telling me the baby wasn't mine, and I trashed the letter, because I simply didn't care. I wanted the nightmare to end. I did not realize that I was throwing away something valuable that could have shed some light on the truth about this woman. Sometimes I wish that I could reach into the past and retrieve that letter. It was so frustrating to deal with this situation; I fell so low, I thought I couldn't get up. I felt like I was the scum of the earth. I was so disgusted with myself, I thought about doing something harsh.

I shared what I was going through with a coworker. He told me that he knew a guy in DC who would have no problem punching Mindy in the stomach, which would make her lose the baby. All I had to do was give a good description and an address. I was disillusioned about the way things had turned out and really upset at the way Mindy was handling this matter. And I was very disgusted with myself for being so naive. I was actually considering his crazy idea. I knew it wasn't right, but I didn't care. But I thank God I had no address and it didn't go down like that, even though I felt like I was getting the wrong end of the stick. But in God's plan I was getting the end of the stick that was right for me. I thought it would have been better if Mindy had taken a contraceptive, we both could have avoided this problem. But I can't put all the blame on her. In fact, I place most of the blame on myself, because I could have protected myself, and I chose not to.

As time went on, I received more papers saying that I had to be in Washington, DC, for a particular court date. I knew that I had to be a man and face reality and handle my responsibilities. My brother Tony and I took the long trip, hoping to see the end of this issue. While we waited for Mindy's arrival, I hoped she would not show, and then someone would see what this woman was about. And sure enough, when it was time, she wasn't there. Later on, I found out she didn't have to be there. But I believe any woman who claims a certain man is her baby's father should be present as well, no exception. But that is a whole different story. When I was standing in front of the judge, he asked if I wanted to take a DNA test. I quickly said yes. I felt like that would be an even better way of showing the court that this woman wasn't right. Right after I left the court, I took the test, but it didn't do any good, because the baby wasn't there to be tested.

The judge ordered me to return to DC. I do not know why. Again, Mindy was not there, and the judge threw out the case and told me never to return to his court again. He made me feel like it was my fault I was in his courtroom. I thought this would be the end of the joke, but the joke was on me. For the third time, I received documents stating that I had to show up in court, this time in North Carolina. I assumed that Mindy had moved back to her hometown. When I first got this news, I was at ease, because I thought that the other cases had been thrown out, and she had nothing else to fight with. But this one would place my balls in a vise and not let go for eighteen years.

I could have prevented this, if only I hadn't been so ignorant. Without knowledge, people perish, so the Bible tells us. Of course, I'd told Tony about this case, and he said I needed to be there. This was the second time my brother gave me great advice, but I took it for granted, which caused me more pain than I anticipated. I was sure I would be in the clear, because the court in DC had dismissed the other case. I did not know that a case thrown out in one state doesn't hold water in another state. And it sucked me into the system like I was dust being sucked into a vent.

I remember Mindy had said she would go out of her way to get even with someone who had done her wrong. I didn't understand how I had done her wrong simply by not bowing down to her demands. Because I didn't do what she wanted, she wanted me to suffer. Believe me, I have. Another incident happened right before I got out of the army. Mindy called the judge advocate general (JAG), the army's lawyers, and they had me sit in their office for hours asking me all kinds of stupid questions. They were trying to prolong my ETS (expiration of term) date by accusing me of violating Article 15 by committing adultery. Mindy told them I was still married and was sleeping with her as well, which was all true on paper. But in reality, I was separated. But thank God for being God, a watchman who overpowers Satan when he gets out of bounds. JAG allowed my superior officer, Sgt. Maj. Wright, to make the decision whether or not to release me. I thought I had served my term, but I was unsure what he would do; he was a very stern man. I thought he wouldn't understand me and would agree with JAG. Sgt. Maj. Wright obviously felt the same way I did, because he had no problem allowing me to be released from the army with an honorable discharge. In fact, he told JAG to let me handle the matter once I got out of the army.

When I got out of the military, the matter was still lingering. I received some more documents stating that I needed to show up at a North Carolina court again. They also stated I could plead my case with a court official because I'd missed the first court date. I did end up talking to a lawyer, who did not care about the problems Mindy was causing me. Mindy didn't show up in North Carolina either; she had someone represent her. I think it is so lame for someone else to show up for the plaintiff, especially when child support is the issue. Nothing should be granted until both parties are present and DNA testing has been carried out. That way no one can get away with anything, and all lies will come to light right then and there.

The North Carolina court transferred the case to Georgia, where I had lived all my life. The court ordered me to pay $1,400 in back child support. I was happy that I didn't have to go to North Carolina, and I thought that someone finally would hear my side of the story and see that something was truly wrong with this woman. Once the date arrived, I went to court and told my side of the story. The judge looked at me as if I were crazy and told me there was nothing he could do. Basically, he said the order had been issued, and I needed to meet the requirements and pay the bill. I didn't have any money, so they locked me up for three days. And if it weren't for my brother Tony getting me out, who knows how long I would have been there. The judge didn't care about the truth, and I know if he wanted to do something, he could have. Until this very day I have paid child support for a child I am not sure is mine. Paying the child support isn't the issue with me, the issue is having a woman that isn't real enough to show up to court and amend what is broken the right way.

I will continue this tale that I wish was a fairy tale at the beginning of my next book. Hopefully, by that time, justice will be served, and the truth will reign. I know that every woman is not manipulative, controlling, cold-blooded, and devious, but these types of women make it harder for the good ones to be trusted. The same is true about men who do crazy things. Mindy and I could have handled this situation like two mature adults. I was willing to make things right, but her plan was totally different from mine. We both were at fault and needed to take full responsibility for our own actions. And the moral of this story for all young men and ignorant men: don't get dragged into the federal system by being stupid. One night of passionate sex cost me all kinds of anguish and unnecessary pain. But I thank God because I could have gone through something much worse, like AIDS. God had to get my attention some way. So if you find yourself caught up, it may help you to become wise and draw near to God. I always tell people, when you think it is bad, it can always get worse.

I saw this child only twice in ten years, and that was after the mother moved to Georgia. The reason she stopped me from seeing my alleged daughter was because, while I was paying her support, I was changing jobs. I made sure that child services had my new job's information, but it took a few weeks for the new job to begin taking out payments. And I won't lie, I was trying to avoid paying it, so I waited until my new employers took it out of my check. It was only a few weeks, but Mindy and I got into an argument about it. And she stopped letting me see the little girl she says is mine. That is what I can't understand; it will never make sense to me.

I know there are some devious men out there in the world; plus, I don't want women to think that I am a male chauvinist. My goal is to understand why some women think a certain way. I can't understand why a woman would accuse a man of having her child, without having a paternity test, and expect this man to pay child support but not let him see his child. If a man is doing what the courts have ordered, it is stupid to stop him from seeing his child. The justice system doesn't care if the woman doesn't let the man visit his child. The only thing they want is the money. The judges say they are for the people, but I can't see how a mess like this is for the people. And women, if you are this type of person, check yourself, because how can you think about being a child of God with your actions. We can't be a nation with dignity unless kids know the truth about who their parents are. I am pretty sure that there are murderers and child molesters who get to visit their kids, with supervision, of course. And I give props to any parent who looks beyond what other people think of them.

# Afterword

I thank everyone who was drawn in by my cover and purchased this book. And I hope it will help you grow into the mature individual that God meant you to be.

The reason I used trees for the chapter titles is because I wanted to do something different. You might ask, what do trees have to do with this book? But I say they are very like human beings. Trees have to go through changes before each season and endure whatever harsh things Mother Nature throws at them. We too have to go through seasons, and we can endure if we learn how to truly trust God.

I dedicate this book to my father, who has passed on into glory. "For I was my father's son, tender and only beloved in the sight of my mother" (Proverbs 4:3). Willie Robinson was a timid man, but he was a wise man as well. He definitely believed in the phrase "spare the rod, spoil the child." For many years, I thought my father didn't love me, until he was gone and I remembered all the valid and important things he did for his children. For example, he moved from a place he thought would have a bad influence on his kids and took us to a small place in the country in Twin City, Georgia. He built a nice brick house for his family. He even had the endurance to stick it out in a difficult marriage until the end. I saw my mother curse my dad out for what I thought was nothing, and he stayed there, with her and their children. My dad loved the saying, "a hard head will make a soft behind," something that I've found out to be very true. I don't know about my other siblings, but my dad didn't spend much time with me, and I couldn't understand that then. But now I know my dad had a lot of responsibilities and a lot on his mind; a person's time can be limited when things are on their mind. He couldn't read or write, but one time he asked me to help him read, and I was excited to help him. We started one day, but it didn't last long; for whatever reason, my dad didn't want to pursue it, and it made me a bit sad. I really wanted my father to do better, and I knew that he could. It depended on him. There was one statement my father would always say; I have no idea where he heard it, but it made more than enough sense. He said, "If I lose my soul, it's nobody's fault but mine." My father may not have showed me love the way my mother did, but he showed it the best way he knew how. He had a remarkable work ethic and hated to be late for work or to miss one day. I love you, Willie Robinson Sr. Rest in peace.